THE MYTH OF THE
JACOBITE CLANS

THE MYTH OF THE JACOBITE CLANS

Murray G. H. Pittock

EDINBURGH UNIVERSITY PRESS

For Ross

© Murray G. H. Pittock, 1995

Edinburgh University Press Ltd
22 George Square, Edinburgh

Typeset in Stempel Garamond
by Pioneer Associates Ltd, Perthshire, and
printed and bound in Great Britain

A CIP record for this book is available
from the British Library

ISBN 0 7486 0715 3

The publisher wishes to
acknowledge subsidy from
the Scottish Arts Council towards
the publication of this volume.

Contents

Acknowledgements

As ever, much is owed to many for this book. Its completion in good time was greatly helped by the granting of leave from Edinburgh University and the Department of English Literature, a leave supported by funding from the British Academy and the University of Aberdeen, through the provision of a Fellowship at the Thomas Reid Institute there in 1994. It was in the November seminar that the main ideas of this work concerning the historical structuring of our understanding of the '45, and the modifications necessary to the way in which we view it, first received a public airing. In particular I should thank George Rousseau, the Director of the Institute, and Joan Pittock Wesson, its former director, now Director of Research. Colin Maclaren was once again very supportive in securing a research grant and, with the aid of his staff, helping me gain access to the Special Collections at Aberdeen: the excellent MacBean Collection there proved a great help, as did the Pitsligo Papers for my work on the political ideas of the 4th Lord Forbes. I should also thank John Gash and Paul Dukes for their help, both academic and social. Nearer home, thanks are owed to the staff of the National Library of Scotland, who enabled me to search the manuscripts pertinaciously, and to my colleagues, particularly Colin Nicholson and Geoffrey Carnall, whose work on the eighteenth century has provided me with valued additional breadth. I am also grateful to the committee of the British Society for Eighteenth-Century Studies, and to Michael Lynch and the Historical Association (Scotland), for providing opportunities to explore the arguments of this book in public, both in London and Edinburgh. Among historians, debts are owed in particular to the work and friendship of Frank McLynn, Jeremy Black, Eveline Cruickshanks, Ross Mackenzie and Bruce Lenman, who helped to set the scholarly stage on which this could be written – through either their work or conversation, and quite often and pleasantly both. Meditating upon the arguments of this and other Jacobite works as a guest on Culloden Moor has a peculiar appropriateness of its own. Most of all, thanks are due to my wife Anne, and, by her persuasion, to our daughters Lexie and Davina for their forbearance. Any faults which follow are my own.

Murray G. H. Pittock
Edinburgh, 1995

INTRODUCTION

British Histories and Scottish Myths

It is astonishing to what an extent the historian has been
Protestant, progressive, and whig . . . Real historical
   understanding is not
achieved by the subordination of the past to the present,
   but rather by
making the past our present.

Herbert Butterfield

On the whole, it was found that the books of the smaller
countries were less biased than those of the great Powers
what English historians have come to call the 'Whig
interpretation of history' has fastened itself too securely
on historical studies in England and elsewhere.

E. H. Dance

'Scientific' pleading is meaningless in principle because the
various value spheres of the world stand in irreconcilable
conflict with one another.

Max Weber

History is always written . . . in the name of a unitary state
apparatus.

Gilles Deleuze[1]

This is a book about Jacobitism. But it is a study with a difference, seeking neither to romanticise its subject nor to demythologise it, but instead to examine the motivations behind the histories which do these things, and to provide further evidence to buttress the revisionist case which has been taking shape over the last twenty years. Its task is twofold: to explain why the Jacobite cause has been (and to an extent still is) so clouded by myth and romanticisation; and to consider in detail the evidence for the nature and extent of Jacobite support among the people of Scotland in the eighteenth century. All the Jacobite risings are considered, but the centre of discussion is the Year of the Prince, 1745–6, as it is here that the clouds of myth are darkest and the romantic light shines brightest. As much as, or more so than, any other movement in British history, the Stuart cause attracts sentimentalists, romantics, 'what if' optimists and debunkers. There are many books from the last school which seek to demythologise Jacobitism; but that is not what is intended here. Rather, it is my contention that Jacobitism has not been demythologised, only remythologised. Those who strive to undermine its myths usually merely offer a different rhetoric of taking sides – which is fundamentally what much of Jacobite history is about: and that itself is interesting. What follows here, then, is not simply a reinterpretation of Jacobitism and the '45: it also assesses the agenda behind the main existing interpretations which we inherit, both romantic and sceptical, showing how both habitually fail to take account of significant facts concerning this Rising. Some of these facts are newly adduced here on the basis of fresh evidence; some have been in circulation, but are often passed over. In Chapters 2 and 3 in particular, I trust they show that our understanding of Jacobitism has often been significantly flawed. Meanwhile, in this Introduction and the following chapter, some of the main interpretations of Jacobite activity come under scrutiny.[2]

One central myth stands as a paradigm for both sceptical and romantic readings: the Myth of the Jacobite Clans. This idea is present in accounts of all the major risings from 1689 to 1745, being powerfully deployed in studies of the last and most famous insurrection. Briefly stated, the Myth of the Jacobite Clans contends that the Jacobite risings (principally the '45) were decidedly peripheral events, based to the north and west of the Highland line, and chiefly supported by a fading civilisation in its Gaelic-speaking and Catholic heartland. Other features of the myth include, on the romantic side, that the '45 was the 'last battle of the Highlanders and the Strangers',[3] that it was a noble, chivalric and doomed attempt by the Children of the Mist who volunteered to restore their Bonnie Prince, and that it was a nationalist rising of Scotland against England. Sceptics, on the other hand, emphasise the marginality of a tribal, Catholic-leaning group unable to come to terms with British society and suggest that the Highlanders were primarily motivated by thieving or had been forced out by self-interested chieftains. It is also said that they did not know what they were fighting for, that more Scots fought against the Jacobites than for them, and that Jacobitism in Scotland was more of a bloody dynastic civil war than a national movement.

Neither these sentiments nor their context are properly supported by a comprehensive examination of the evidence, but this is not their purpose. Taking sides is at the core of the Jacobite issue, which is why we should always beware of 'neutrality'. The full tale of the Stuart cause remains too often untold, despite a huge number of tellers: it is, as I hope to show, a historical narrative controlled by political need. After the 1994 release of the film *Chasing the Deer*, Tom Nairn and Peter Clarke clashed over its relevance in the pages of *The Scotsman*. Each saw in it nothing to challenge their own beliefs, which is a tribute to a film which presents an essentially sceptical reading of Jacobitism while endeavouring not to displease the romantics too greatly: for example, the Prince's conduct at Culloden is given as benevolent a portrayal as humanly possible. 'Do you think I would have wanted it zis way?' he lisps in an appalling French accent made more galling by the Received Pronunciation of a Duke of Cumberland, whose family retained traces of German intonation up till the reign of Edward VII; but, on the other hand, Charles Edward does not lose his temper, accuse Lord George Murray of treachery, blame everyone but himself and prophesy his own defeat. By presenting a largely acceptable romanticised Prince amid a sceptical reading of the '45, *Chasing the Deer* attempts to balance its audience in an equal but opposite way to that sought by the National Trust for Scotland, which presents a romantic reading of the 1745 Rising (a 'last battle' for Gaelic civilisation) in tandem with a sceptical one of the Prince in its 1984 slideshow at Culloden.[4]

As suggested above, it is my contention that sceptical and romantic readings share more than what divides them, in the sense that both are myths. Rather than relying on what has been called the 'logos (demonstrable truth)' of history, they are producers and inheritors of the need for 'mythos (authoritative pronouncement)' concerning it.[5] The 'authoritative pronouncement' which they seek is fundamentally one of interpretation rather than fact, the manifesto of one side of the argument, dependent more on ridicule than demonstration in undermining its opponents. Such history has been seen, like myth itself which rests in a heartland of repeated stories, as 'existence . . . valorized by the repetition of archetypal gestures'. As I shall show, the history of Jacobitism is full of the 'repetition of archetypal gestures' on both sides: gestures which do little more than restate a *parti pris*. The mythic quality of Jacobitism is demonstrated both in the repetition of romantic gestures and images concerning it, and in the context of attempts at demythologising it, which attempts, through their frequency, bear about them the marks of cultural gesturing. Both are allied in that both draw on a continual fascination with the subject characteristic of myth. One of myth's functions is to provide provisional explanations for an issue where passion, ignorance or simply the human condition prevent the ordering force of a rational settlement from prevailing: and this is the case with Jacobitism. Over the years, the condition of Britain, more particularly of British history, has often had an interest in rendering elusive 'demonstrable truth' as it affects the Jacobite case.

Whig history is the main vehicle for a primarily sceptical mythologising of Jacobitism. Since Herbert Butterfield wrote in 1931, the end of such history has been prematurely proclaimed. Whig history is essentially a history which conditions its interpretation of the past by what it has produced in the present: it is thus quintessentially a history written to glorify victors and marginalise losers, in the process writing a narrative whose ultimate end is the explanation and through that the justification of whatever society is its present. In Britain, confronted with a multinational state, it has, in Gilles Deleuze's terms, sought to confirm the genesis of 'a unitary state apparatus'. E. H. Dance's 1967 argument in his report on 'Bias in History Teaching' to the Centre for Cultural Co-operation of the Council of Europe was that 'the universities have already freed themselves' from this tradition, which only remained central in school textbooks. Whether or not this was over-optimistic, the Jacobite movement, one of the central battlegrounds of Whig history, has certainly benefited greatly in the last twenty-five years (and intermittently before this) from the work of many gifted revisionists. What Daniel Szechi defines in his 1994 book *The Jacobites* as the 'optimist' and 'pessimist' outlook on Jacobitism are alike born from a new understanding of at least its potential importance, whereas the 'rejectionist' school are the inheritors of the traditional historiography which pushed Jacobitism to the margin. Nevertheless, despite such developments in the debate, the traditional accounts of Jacobitism's marginality are deeply grounded in British history, as we shall see. Even at the forefront of scholarship, Whig history remains powerful and prominent today at the highest levels. For example, Linda Colley's *Britons* (1992) comes to certain conclusions about Protestant solidarity and the marginality of the Stuarts which are more than redolent of the pages of that Whig doyen, Macaulay. In the words of James Young, 'Colley's book reflects the Anglocentric bias of the Oxbridge school of history from above', and one of the achievements of revisionist Jacobite history has been to link its subject to some of the illuminating evidence recovered from a history from below.[6]

Romantic readings of Jacobitism, on the other hand, ultimately do nothing to challenge the sceptics, because they accept the marginalisation and detachment of the Jacobite past from the mainstream of historical development. Not only do they present the Stuart cause as high drama of a colourful kind: they also implicitly show it as doomed to fail. It is also almost always detached from its international perspective: far from Jacobitism being a movement with widespread sympathy and support in Europe, it becomes a struggle of loyal Highlanders alone to restore their injured prince. Context-free, romantic Jacobitism idealises a past from which it secretly celebrates its detachment, as Hugh MacDiarmid saw.[7]

Although romantic and sceptical explications of the Myth of the Jacobite Clans are found at their most flagrant in popular history, their endurance there is possible because scholarly history itself frequently continues to perpetuate a narrative of inherited orthodoxy. The process whereby the development of scholarship percolates down to popular accounts is largely absent from Jacobitism, because the powerful and habitual misrepresentation of the Stuart cause still has many friends at all levels of historical analysis: Keynes's view that 'common sense' in economics may only be servitude to the obsolescent ideas of some defunct economist is not inapposite.[8]

The Myth of the Jacobite Clans remains at the core of both sides of the mythologising process. There are a number of motivations responsible for its continuing centrality. First, and chiefly, it marginalises Jacobitism by uniting its political aims and their expression to a culture characterised as declining and peripheral, if not simply uncivilised and savage. By attaching the Stuart cause so firmly to an extinct mode of social organisation with a failing language, the historian, particularly the Whig historian seeking to provide a teleology for the present which forbids the defeated movements of the past enduring relevance, reinforces a strong picture of a dying and doomed cause. Such a definitive marginality can also be useful to the romantic who wishes to depict much the same material with much the same message in a history which could only ever have had one outcome, but seeks also to celebrate the loyalty, bravery and heroic Celtic fortitude of those who fought and always fell. Both interpretations associated Jacobitism with a strongly demarcated Highland/Lowland divide, a reactionary and often Catholic world-view, headstrong and bloodthirsty magnate chieftains and all the other weeds firmly rooted in the traditional account of an old Scotland full of overmighty subjects who must be subdued before the progressive and beneficial victory of commercial civil society can take place: what Colin Kidd in a recent article calls 'the legend of late medieval Scotland as a benighted magnate anarchy'. Thus the Stuart cause becomes a 'history at the margin'. In so becoming, it enters a state of heritage – defining 'heritage' as historical events which have ceased to have contemporary relevance, and in so doing have transmuted themselves into artefacts to be owned and revisited by a present and future no longer attached to them by the live links of political consequence.[9]

The importance of heritage to British identity in the last 200 years, more particularly (as will be discussed in Chapter 1) in the last century, is the second central reason for the Myth of the Jacobite Clans. It succeeds in enshrining them as a romantic curio which evokes the loyalty and battleworthiness of the Highlanders while displaying them as part of an extinct society, an extinct society whose motivations and beliefs are detached from ours almost as if it belonged to a different country. Jacobitism, linked to that society, is separated from British politics: which is why a heritage reading of Jacobitism is also motivated towards the primary characterisation of the Stuart cause in Highland terms. Seen as a broad-based phenomenon within the Scottish polity, Jacobitism would be too closely tied to national identity, and with it nationalism. Sometimes the romantic side of the heritage reading accepts Jacobitism as a kind of nationalism, one of the 'clans who fought for Scotland and Prince Charlie', to quote the Culloden monument. But the important point to recall here is that the nationalism of such Jacobitism is that of a nation, 'the clans', which is now effectively extinct. Hence the 'Scotland' of Jacobitism is, to paraphrase Marlowe, another country, and besides the cause is dead. In emphasising that the '45 was a peripheral event and that the 'modern' part of Scotland resisted it, a construct is produced which forces Jacobitism to the edge of historical narration, keeping it from troubling us further save as an *aide-mémoire* to sentiment. For example, the tourist industry which protects both heritage and the sentiment which it recalls to us appears to dictate that on Culloden Moor the Hanoverian line of battle should be described in terms of regiments, the Jacobite one in terms of clans. The emphasis here is threefold: first, it renders the Jacobite army marginal and more akin to a ragbag of militia than a conventional force (the regimental order books show it was the latter); second, that marginality serves to emphasise the doomed yet chivalric role of the whole enterprise; and third, tourist sentiment is stirred by encouraging visitors to 'recognise' their 'families' among the graves and battlefield memorials to the clans. In this way, a domestic, essentially Kailyard veneer is given to an international political movement: families fight regiments. How brave, how foolish, how sad.[10]

Marginality and the sentimental romance of heritage both link with primitivism, a third motivation behind the myth. The Highland account of the nature of Jacobitism was, as we shall see, well served by the eighteenth-century development of primitivism and its Romantic connections, which idealised the Highlander in noble savage vein. The affection which heritage conceives for a history that its consumers are relieved to know is remote is echoed in the seductively romantic side of primitivism, with its reportage of tragic finales to an ancient way of life that few of its admirers would care to practise, such as is found in the work of James Macpherson, discussed in Chapter 1. The primitivist mode of interpretation, while offering a superficially flattering account of the Highland role in Jacobitism, lends itself readily to marginalisation and distancing.[11]

There are two other motivating causes for the Myth which seem more bound up with confusion and inadequate emphasis than with mythologising per se. The first is the inadequate distinction made between the Highlands and the rest of Scotland north of the Forth in some Jacobite history. This confusion, as I attempt to show in Chapter 2, has its roots not only in contemporary accounts of the 1745 Rising, but also in the policy adopted by the Jacobite leadership during that Rising, of using Highland dress as a uniform for the troops in general – a policy which will be seen to offer an interesting commentary on the exact nature of a Jacobite 'Highlander'. The second reason is a simple one of inadequate emphasis: many accounts virtually forget the presence of a second army in Scotland during Charles Edward's march on London, and those that mention it seldom analyse its composition. The 4000 men (6000 by Jacobite estimates, and a possible grand total, though far more than the number of effectives) defending the east-coast Lowlands at the end of 1745 were, with the exception of Lieutenant-General Lord John Drummond's 800–1100 Franco-Scots and Irish troops, heavily Lowland by origin. There may also have been a tendency, discussed further in Chapter 2, for Lowland troops to serve closer to their place of recruitment. Given that the glamour of the campaign rests chiefly on the capture of Edinburgh, the battle of Prestonpans and the march to Derby, it has thus been easy for both romantics and sceptics only to touch on or even to ignore some of the spheres of Lowland recruitment.[12]

The above five reasons I believe to be the root motivations for a historical view which is still over-inclined to emphasise the Highland nature of Jacobitism. In doing so, both sentimental and cynical accounts marginalise their subject, while through rote repetition of unexamined shibboleths set within a conventional narrative, they confirm for their stories the status of myth. Before describing how this myth will be tackled in the ensuing chapters, I now turn to examine examples of emphasis in the history which has been here accused.

Although English supporters of the government in 1745 were quite likely to suspect that all Scots were disloyal, the habitual depiction of Scots as Highlanders in the political cartoon tradition appears to have become blended with comments such as that of a leading Whig decision-maker, who described the forces opposing the state as '5 or 6000 Highlanders' to create an idea reflected in the 1745 set of 'Lillibullero' that 'an army's just coming without any shoes' out of a marginal wilderness to threaten 'Court, country and city'. Distinctions between the Gaeltachd and the rest of Scotland were blurred – a process which often occurs in the characterisation of 'margins' by 'centres'. Prints such as *Sawney in the Boghouse*, which showed Scots as too stupid to use the lavatory, gave a distinctive eighteenth-century edge to traditional depictions of lice-ridden cannibalism. (Interestingly, the idea of Scots as cannibals, apocryphally realised in the legend of Sawney Bean, was also found in eighteenth-century English chapbook literature about the West Country: in such remote margins, what other kind of behaviour could be expected? This smear was of course exported to Africa in the colonial age.) In the 1740s, government and pro-government propaganda presented a peripheral and primitive view of the Jacobites in order to emphasise their barbarism and its irrelevance.[13]

This is not remarkable; what is remarkable is the endurance of this depiction, beginning in the distancing of Jacobitism practised by Lowland Scots keen to show their loyalty in the 1750s and 1760s. One of the arguments used for a Scottish militia in the Seven Years' War was that without it, Lowland Scotland had been defenceless against the northern caterans in 1745 (and this was taken up by nineteenth-century historians such as Charles Macfarlane); in Chapter 2 we will see how far this accords with the facts. Later historians continued and amplified the distancing of Jacobitism from the main thoroughfare of historical needs and development. G. M. Trevelyan, for example, describes the Highlanders as 'barbarians' in a Scotland where, indistinguishably, 'the age of barbarism was at last coming to an end' by the close of the seventeenth century (just in time for the benefits of Union). Charles's army in 1745 is described as '5000 Highlanders' engaged in the pursuit of 'a fantasia of misrule . . . in defiance of Parliament and the laws . . . Parliamentary government . . . could scarcely have survived the repeal of fundamental statutes by kilted swordsmen'. Describing the relationship between Edinburgh and the areas of Jacobite support in the aftermath, Trevelyan observes that 'an Afghanistan could no longer be tolerated within fifty miles of the "modern Athens"'. The classic Whig polarity between the 'fundamental statutes' of the constitution and the so-called 'tribal swordsmen' of intrusive barbarity could, one might think, hardly be more pronounced than this. But in fact the 'Afghanistan' analogy is quite moderate. Charles Chevenix Trench, writing in 1973, describes the Jacobites as 'a savage Highland horde, as alien . . . as a war party of Iroquois', opposed by 'English and Lowland troops' alike. In this assessment, perhaps Trench was merely following Justin McCarthy, who in his *History of the Four Georges* sees the 'clansmen, as savage and as desperately courageous as Sioux or Pawnees' (they also have an impossible language, since Charles attempts 'the desperate task of trying to master the Gaelic speech'). Bruce Lenman, in his *Jacobite Clans of the Great Glen*, notes the irony of

Highlanders characterised in such terms (as they effectively had been since the '45) being used to fight the American Indians in the Seven Years' War. However, the Native Americanisation of the Gaeltachd can be traced in at least one Jacobite, Colonel John, Master of Sinclair, who not only grumbles about the fondness for tartan shown by at least one of his Lowland compatriots in 1715, but also asks 'What does an Iroquois, a Negre, a Laplander, a Scots Western Islander, yea, a Highlandman think of? Is it not hunting, fishing, stealeing, plundering and revenging themselves of their enemies?' The Master, who had been expelled from the British Army for killing two men, was evidently of a superior temper. He, however, was far from identifying the Jacobite cause as Highland, marginal and colonial, since he appears to have wished as few Highlanders as possible to be associated with the restoration of the Stuarts, and was more or less the only Jacobite with such views. [14]

Even where the analysis is less strident, the effect is similar. Basil Williams in *The Whig Supremacy* tells us that 'the Highlanders' were defeated at Culloden; J. R. Green in *A Short History of the English People* says that though the Prince was at the 'head of six thousand men' after Prestonpans, 'all were still Highlanders, for the people of the Lowlands held aloof from his standard', while Cassell's *History of the British People*, remarks of this 'romantic episode' that 'a dozen clans, a few Lowland gentlemen, a few ruined adventurers and exiles' (note how the Highlanders are counted by 'clan' and any others only as individuals) supported it. Samuel Gardiner, while acknowledging Edinburgh as an exception, suggests that 'in Scotland the traders . . . were Hanoverians to a man'. In sceptical mode, Dicey and Rait proclaim that 'the Lowlanders were mostly Whigs and the clansmen, guided by loyalty to their chiefs, were hardly Jacobites'. A. D. Innes, on the Primitivist-Romantic side, writes of the 'chivalry', 'loyalty' and 'audacity' which 'had actually brought some six thousand clansmen from the wild Highlands of Scotland within measurable distance of winning back the British crown for the House of Stuart'. This is a more positive reading than Sir Winston Churchill's view of the Highlanders 'Living in their mountain villages like hill tribesmen . . . the immemorial zest for plunder . . . still unslaked', but the two accounts mainly diverge only in the degree of sentimentality or cynicism they severally bring to bear on what both agree is a remote and antiquated culture. Another Romanticist piece, James Michael Hill's *Celtic Warfare*, published in 1986, similarly does no favours in describing 'the attack against all reason, against all odds' which was the hallmark of 'primitive peoples' of the Celtic lands, though at least he acknowledges that not all the Jacobite army in 1745 were Highlanders. Robert Rayner in *A Concise History of Britain* backs up the idea of hopeless odds, when he decrees 'the Highland clans' to have been in pursuit of 'such a forlorn hope' (and its 'forlorn' quality is the reason that the (sensible) English did not join). McCarthy likewise spices up his sceptical reading with a dose of patronising romance: 'the Young Chevalier's troops ... believed, in the wild Gaelic way, in the sanctity of their cause'. Whereas Keith Feiling approaches a perceived lack of Lowland support in the '45 with caution, Charles Macfarlane in his *Comprehensive History of England* states that 'the majority ... of Edinburgh' were 'wishing every "sharp-edged claymore man" behind Strathbogie' (unsurprisingly, if the Highlanders were motivated by poverty as he suggests). Macfarlane sneers at the appointment of a 'quarter-master-general – an office scarce needed in a Highland army', though he admits that the army contained men from 'that part of Scotland which lies nearest the Highlands' – but then most of it does. In fact, as the surviving regimental order books show, the army was remarkably conventional in its organisation, and was more than a 'Highland' 'raid' in 'a year of romantic vicissitudes', to quote Sir Fitzroy Maclean and Sir George Clark's histories. It also possessed very able military leaders: leaving Lord George Murray aside, at least two of the other senior commanders reached general officer level in continental armies (Lieutenant-Generals Lords Ogilvy and Drummond in France), while the more junior Allan Maclean reached that rank locally in the British Army in Canada, despite leading his regiment into battle wearing white cockades, to the irritation of his superiors. The Master of Lovat, who admittedly took little active part in the 1745 Rising, also became a British general, while William Sharp, great-grandson of the Archbishop of St

Andrews murdered on Magus Moor, became a major-general in the Portuguese service.[15]

The sentiments quoted above, ranging from standard to school histories, are no longer at the cutting edge of Jacobite scholarship (although some come from books published recently). Yet historical revisionism has made surprisingly little impact on some of the leading accounts published in the last twenty years, for the end of Whig history is more promised than performed. Paul Langford in *A Polite and Commercial People* (1989) passes on without comment the view that 1745 saw 'the preservation of England against a Highland rabble', while more surprising still is Linda Colley's statement in her acclaimed *Britons* (1992) that 'only the poorer Highland clans . . . rallied to the Young Pretender' in Scotland. Colley's view that 'the centrality of trade . . . helped to ensure that the rejection of the Jacobite option was decisive' and that this led to 'negligible civilian support' echoes R. H. Campbell's earlier judgement in *Scotland Since 1707*: how far it is true of Scotland we shall see. Annette Smith, writing in 1988, calls the northern army at Dundee 'the occupying Highland force', though she is discussing Lowland recruitment there (such apparent doublethink is not uncommon, so deep is the notion of a 'Highland Army' ingrained). This extends to separating Jacobite political aims from political behaviour characterised as 'Lowland'. For example, J. G. A. Pocock, apostle of a supposedly fairer 'four nations' British history, appears to see the conquest of the Highlands after 1745 as resulting from the 'lowland kingdom's' having sought 'an incorporating union' which bound it to North British loyalties (support for the Union in fact declined rapidly down the social scale below the peerage in Scotland: it was conservatively acknowledged that three-quarters of the population at the time were against it, and there were far higher estimates). Although Daniel Szechi (with Geoffrey Holmes) has provided a more balanced account of Jacobite patriotism in Scotland in the 'four nations' survey *The Age of Oligarchy*, 'four nations' British history, no matter how fair it claims to be, does not always interrogate the sources which would help it to be so: for example, Alistair and Henrietta Tayler, after 'careful investigation', constructed very full lists of hundreds of Lowland Jacobites from Aberdeen and Banffshire alone more than half a century ago.[16]

There are perhaps two wellsprings to be taken account of in our understanding of this selective admissions policy on the part of British history: what E. H. Carr once revealingly described as the 'club' of historical facts. First, until recently, 'Britain' as an entity had long been unchallenged – and as Britons, we owe the greatest historical debt to an identity which marginalised Jacobitism in order to remove its dynastic, political and Scottish and Irish nationalist dimensions. On this reading, it is thus no coincidence that strongly revisionist Jacobite scholarship has become widespread at almost exactly the same time as modern political nationalism has made an impression on these islands. Not that it is at all the case that such revisionist scholarship is nationalist: the majority of it is not so, but the point is that its availability has something to do with the way in which we view our own cultural certainties. Attacks on the central myths of Whig historiography are part and parcel of this process, though it is a powerful survivor in our consciousness of the general shape of history.[17]

Whereas the cultural causes of historical revisionism may remain somewhat speculative, much clearer evidence is available in confirmation of the second cause of Highlandisation: the confused and blurred boundaries between the Gaeltachd and the rest of Scotland, which date back to pro-government propaganda in the '45, and which were taken advantage of by Sir Walter Scott for romanticising purposes in his rendering Scotland a nation of Highlanders for George IV's 1822 visit, as one of the northern wizard's discommoded countrymen complained. In this context, even distinguished Scottish historians can show signs of a fundamentally romantic confusion between Scotland and the Gaeltachd. Despite going on to say (quite rightly) that the Jacobites 'drew strength from two main areas – the central and western Highlands and the north-east Lowland plain' and (more doubtfully, as I shall show in Chapter 2) that Highland troops volunteered whereas Lowlanders were forced, William Ferguson, in his landmark work *Scotland: 1689 to the Present*, can nonetheless state that

An account of . . . recruitment and organisation emphasises the great social and economic cleavages that divided Britain at that period. Nowhere else in the British Isles could such a force have been assembled, for only in the Highlands of Scotland . . . were martial attributes still the stuff of everyday life. There is nothing 'romantic' in such a bald statement of well-attested fact. Sir Walter Scott in *Waverley*, the greatest of his novels, so far as history is concerned invented little.

On the contrary, as recent scholarship has demonstrated, Scott invented a great deal, not least, as Colin Kidd says, 'by applying a sentimental Jacobite gloss to basic Whig constitutionalism' (1994, 7). Indeed, there is a great deal of pure romanticising in this 'bald' and 'well-attested fact', both in the Highlandisation of the 1745 Rising here indulged in, and also in what, as for example Frank McLynn points out, is an idealisation of a clan system on the whole more given to self-interest than the Episcopalian ideologues of the Lowlands. The mention of 'social and economic cleavages' seems to be an implicit confirmation of the traditional view that the commercial classes eschewed the Rising.[18]

The definition of 'Highland' and 'Highlander' in this book endeavours to avoid the more serious aspects of confusion between the Gaeltachd and other parts of Scotland, while recognising that there are distinctions between different parts of the Highlands as well as differing levels of cultural distinction in eighteenth-century Scotland which did not always follow a Highland/Lowland divide. In the ensuing pages, the term 'Highlander' generally refers to a Jacobite living north-west of the Highland line, though the special status of areas contiguous to the Highlands is also acknowledged. For example, in the assessment of the strength of Lowland Jacobitism, the mixed nature of the Atholl Brigade and other units is accepted.

In Chapter 1, I go on to discuss the specific kinds of historical misrepresentation found in both sceptical and romantic attempts at Jacobite mythologising. In Chapter 2, the level and sources of Jacobite support in the major risings are evaluated, while Chapter 3 examines the evidence in one of the main zones of contention between the various mythologies of Jacobitism: mediating between the views that the cause and its leaders were simply exploiting Scottish society in a dynastic war, or were romantic nationalists engaged in a struggle with the British state. Chapter 4 discusses the issue of Jacobitism's historic role in Scottish culture: both romantic Jacobitism's development into a set of products and a heritage industry, and the political use of images of Jacobitism in nationalist and unionist interpretations of identity. Some concluding suggestions are made regarding the most useful and accurate way of viewing a topic still so controversial, as well as a major source of the irritating or comforting productions of kitsch.

James MacKnight, the thoughtful nineteenth-century editor of the memoirs of John, Master of Sinclair, wrote that 'each author apparently decides in accordance with his own personal predilections' the strength of Jacobitism and its support; and it may be objected that the present author will do no more than take sides after the time-honoured fashion. There is no avoidance of some bias, and all bias damages truth. But to damage truth is not the same thing as to promote myth: the distinction between 'demonstrable truth' and the repeated, reinforcing and unexamined pronouncements of myth alluded to above is a real one. The central problem of the Myth of the Jacobite Clans lies not so much in bias with regard to a comprehensive examination of the facts, as in a suppression of the readily demonstrable in the interests of the partisan. Jacobitism may have stood no hope of success irrespective of the fact that it had extensive Lowland support and that Cumberland did not command more Scots at Culloden than did the Prince (for example); but what we need to know is why there is repeated reinforcement of accounts which on the whole do not examine the 1745 Rising with much care, though it is written of endlessly. Challenging partisan myths is more important than the bias which this study will undoubtedly show, though I hope that bias will not be unreasonable in the context of Jacobitism's European status in the eighteenth century. For example, James is called 'James VIII and III' in recognition of the acceptance of his title at the time, and George I is not thereby termed the Elector of Hanover, though he certainly held that office. Charles Edward is termed 'prince' at every date, since he was not recognised as 'king' by the range of powers which accorded his father that title. This use is intended to display Jacobitism's status as a European dynastic controversy, although this study itself concentrates on Scotland.[19]

Problems in the use of sources have undoubtedly helped to promote the partisan qualities of the myth. Sceptical historians have had difficulties with the absence of reliable documentation for much Jacobite activity which, even where it exists, has seemed blighted by overblown optimism and unreliable supposition. At the same time, the tradition of seeking out the central documents of power rather than marginal accounts has not helped either: if 'Power constitutes the essential theme of political history', then the efforts of those who never (re)gained it must take second place. The 'strolling minstrels and pedlars of stories', somewhat rehabilitated as historical source material since Butterfield celebrated the historian's appropriation of their role sixty years ago, are central not only to the culture of Jacobitism but to the very distribution of Jacobite propaganda. In Hayden White's terms, an 'ironic consciousness of its own formal nature' has generally failed to penetrate the centralising and centralist narratives of British history, which have thus accommodated Jacobitism in the marginalised and mythicising manner outlined above. Such distancing is appropriately relieved only by an ironic consciousness of the limitations of the historian's structures.[20]

While the problems of provisionality cannot be altogether evaded, thorough gathering of evidence can to an extent accumulate empirical standards of truth. In pursuit of that, I shall draw on various kinds of documentary support. The account in Chapter 1 bases itself on discussion of some of the underlying prejudices and myths in British history, and conducts its argument mostly, if not entirely, through a range of secondary sources. The second chapter compares and synthesises available accounts of Jacobite support, drawing also on contemporary intelligence reports and statements made after the 1745 Rising; the third chapter brings together Episcopalian political and literary writing with Stuart declarations in pursuit of the ideology of Scottish Jacobitism. Thus the contemporary views of Jacobites and Whigs at all levels are used, and hostile witnesses are often cited when dealing with the strength of Lowland Jacobitism.

I attempt to retrieve (where available) the dimensions and intensity of Jacobite support viewed from a number of sources, many of which are rarely if ever cited. Continuing interest in Jacobitism needs to be met not just by a repetition of what has gone before, but through an analysis of the nature of such repetition, scrutinised afresh from a range of evidence taken across the culture and society of the time. This is part of the revisionist project, but is also an extension of both its means and ends. If this discussion is at all successful in its quest to, in Rosalind Mitchison's words, 'disturb the accepted myths', it will have helped to give a fresh perspective on Jacobitism and ourselves in relation to it, more than 250 years since the '45 began.[21]

CHAPTER I

Children of the Mist

The qualities which render English political and religious institutions the freest in the world are an inheritance from Germanic forefathers . . . the dedication to George I of his [Edmund Gibson, Bishop of Lincoln and later of London] translation of Camden's *Britannica* glows with pride in the common Saxon origin which linked the Hanoverian king with his English subjects . . . if we enquire from whence our Saxon ancestors came, we shall find, that it was from your Majesty's dominions in Germany.

Hugh MacDougall

[S]ince the early seventeenth century Irish historians had been working to overthrow the arguments of Sir John Davies (1569–1626) which justified English conquest and colonial reconstruction of Irish society on the grounds of Celtic barbarity.

Colin Kidd

But if the white rose of the Stuarts had faded forever in blood, the lost race, in him, their last and greatest hero [Charles], had reached its immortality – enshrined forever in the pages of romance, endeared to all generous hearts in the realms of song.

W. Blaikie Murdoch

The Gael . . . had gone forth in the quest of a dream . . . spoilt
children of the mist . . . were they not indeed Romance per-
sonified! . . . born with the fairies' gift of second sight, and a
little handful of gladness wherewith to outweigh the evil of
things.

Pittendrigh Macgillavray[1]

The impact which English nationalism has had on the shaping of
British identity is central to our understanding of the Myth of
the Jacobite Clans in both romantic and sceptic forms: 1745 was
after all the last mainland attempt to overthrow the British state, in
its modernising and centripetal form, and at least one distinguished
eighteenth-century historian (Jeremy Black) has adjudged it the
most serious military threat faced by the country in that century. In
this context it is important to remember that in 1745 Britain was
still a nascent state, engaged in developing itself in ways which
inevitably leant heavily on English cultural experience. Ernest
Gellner has argued that nationalism is 'the inseparable *ideological
counterpart of modernization*'; and while there may be space to
question this as a universal definition, it is undoubtedly the case
that the 1745 Rising is central to the modernising narrative of Anglo-
British history. Occurring on the brink of the Enlightenment, the
last great Jacobite struggle is in some respects pictured as the battle
between a conservative agrarian society and its commercial industrial replacement (despite the status of many leading Jacobites as
improvers): indeed, this model fits Gellner's later construct of the
displacement of the agrarian phase of human society rather well.
The mythic nature of conventional accounts of the 1745 Rising
also confirms Gellner's view that '*logical and social coherence are
inversely related*'. By this analysis, the long-standing marginalisation of the '45 is part of its function within the narrative of British
history: it must become futile and of little threat in order to confirm
the victory of Hanoverian modernity more fully. The coherence of
Britain thus demands that certain facts about the Rising are also
marginalised, as derogating from the traditional historical perspective on British national and social solidarity (e.g. both Scottish
nationalist and middle-class support for the Jacobites receive little
attention). At the same time, Jacobite principle and loyalty can be

viewed in a romantic light as the misplaced precursor of the military function of Scottish, particularly Highland Scottish, troops within the British Empire.[2]

As I have argued elsewhere, there are two major themes through which Anglo-British nationalism finds expression. The first can be called the imperial register of nationhood; the second the organic register. The imperial register posits a common enemy (externally often France, internally Catholicism or the marginal 'barbarity' of Scots and Welsh Celts) in order to generate national cohesion 'in response to conflict with the Other', to quote Linda Colley. In Edmund Burke's definition of that 'Other', 'Every thing we have done is in the style of hostility to France, as a nation': it was thus no coincidence that the major consolidations of English rule within the British Isles ('1689, 1707, 1745, 1801') were 'taken in the context of Anglo-French warfare'. England's power within Britain was consolidated by opposition to France. Particularly during the period and aftermath of these victories, imperial nationalism could voice itself in terms of seapower and its associated effects (as Linda Colley notes, in 'Rule Britannia' it is 'Britain's supremacy *offshore* which is being celebrated', the ruling of the waves), the uniqueness of the constitution and the Church of England, the alien nature of Roman Catholicism, racial mythology (Saxon stolidity and Celtic fire, the immaturity, folly and plain ridiculousness of foreigners), and, above all, the idea of the British as uniquely 'born to liberty' by a series of fortunate constitutional developments linked to the genetic predisposition of the Gothic races, engines of a progress fuelled by the history which it surpassed. In this context, it becomes possible to describe Scots in the aftermath of the Jacobite risings as ethnically Germanic for constitutional purposes, and Celticised for military ones. Hence the Scot (after the 1760s, at any rate) was now ethnically predisposed to British liberty, while his Celtic impurities could purge their noble savagery in war against those other 'primitive' races who required to be educated into the *Pax Britannica*: thus there is a strong military bias in positive Celtic images of Scotland, such as Sir Walter Scott prepared for George IV's visit in 1822. Hence also came the continuing characterisation of those whose knowledge of liberty needed development in animal, infantile or adolescent terms in nineteenth-century writing about the colonies or the Highlands.[3]

Complications in the British Empire and its eventual contraction and virtual disappearance began to compromise the success of the imperial register of British patriotism from the late nineteenth century onwards. As a result, increasing priority was given in patriotic imagery to organic rhetoric, a typification of British identity by what sort of place the country is rather than by what role it has. Though of ancient origin, organic conceptualisations of Britishness had not been central in the eighteenth and nineteenth centuries, partly perhaps because of their association with the ideology of Stuart ruralism and the Jacobite leanings of many 'country' lairds and gentry, and partly due to the strong emphasis on state-building in the period. In the twentieth century, Stanley Baldwin voices the nostalgic sweep of organic Britishness in typical vein:

> The sounds of England, the tinkle of the hammer on the anvil in a country smithy, the corncrake on a dewy morning, the sound of the scythe against the whetstone, and the sight of a plough team coming over the brow of the hill, the sight . . . seen in England since England was a land . . . the one eternal sight of England . . .

as does John Major sixty-seven years later:

> Britain in fifty years will still be the country of long shadows on county grounds, warm beer, invincible green suburbs, dog lovers, and – as George Orwell said – old maids bicycling to Holy Communion through the morning mist – Britain will survive unamendable in all essentials.

As can be seen from the above, the organic register shows Britain as rural or small-town, agricultural, quiet and overwhelmingly southern English in historic inheritance and cultural practice. Although an increasingly ridiculous portrayal even of these realities, it has had widespread influence this century, particularly in advertising, popular culture and the cult of the countryside.[4]

As suggested above, imperial versions of identity predominate in the Jacobite period. A 1762 cartoon on the Earl of Bute's ministry portrays a poor John Bull with cuckold's horns, ridden by a Scotland which is secretly taking gold proffered by a French monkey, thus illustrating both imperial paranoia and the manner in which Scotland, fifty-five years after the Union, was hardly better integrated into the Anglo-British world-view than was France, England's ancient hereditary enemy. Anti-Scottish and anti-Jacobite propaganda (there was often little distinction) showed Scots as ill-fed, ill-dressed, loutish and verminous. The French, frequently depicted in alliance with the Scots in Jacobite times, were similarly depicted as ragged and underfed in the French Revolutionary period. Nor was the political message (as opposed to the means of its depiction) of anti-Jacobite propaganda entirely irrelevant or inaccurate. Pro-Jacobite writing in Scotland was at the same time lamenting the lost Union which the country 'had of late with France' (in the time of Queen Mary): such Francophilia was a gift to British propaganda. The categorisation of Jacobitism as 'foreign', therefore outré, marginal, inferior and quite probably Catholic and malign, was frequent and telling: in addition to France and Scotland, Italy, when it became the residence of both the Stuarts and the papacy, was a gift to Jacobitism's detractors. This was a neat response to Jacobite xenophobia directed against the Dutch and later the Germans. It was thus perhaps largely in vain that English and Lowland Scottish Jacobites appropriated patriotic Highlander iconography (of which more shortly) in reply: the 'charlie' fir trees, tartan waistcoats and so on of the defiant Jacobite gentry could not have been as powerful as the repeated associations of Jacobitism with what was un-English. This even went to the extent of giving James VIII and III a fake Gaelic accent in one verse satire, while in another of the 1690s his status as Prince of Wales is deliberately confused with ethnic Welshness, to render him a Celtic buffoon. The Welsh hardly had a better profile than the Scots or French, as is evinced in the eighteenth-century chapbook 'The Pleasant History of TAFFY's Progress to London; with the WELSHMAN's Catechism':

> The much renowned Taffy William Morgan receiv'd a Letter sent by word of Mouth from London [i.e. he cannot read] which gave him an Account how Despisable the poor

Welshman claims Britains were made in England on Saint Tafy's day, by the Rabble hanging out a Bundle of Rags in representation of a Welshman mounted on a Red Herring with a Leek in his Hat, truly poor Morgan's Blood was up ['my Welsh blood's up' exclaims James, Prince of Wales in an anti-Jacobite verse satire], he Fretted and Fum'd till he Foam'd at Mouth Agen, and being exuspirated [sic] as much as the French King was Joyful when he first heard of the great Victory obtain'd by Marshal Tallard over the Duke of Marlborough at Hochstet, he in a great Passion swore by the Glory and Renown of all his Ancestors, famous in the Books of Rates for their ever being chargeable to the Parish, that he would be Reveng'd on those that thus presumed to affront Goatlandshire . . .⁵

All the features of marginalisation found in more sophisticated historical narratives are in place here. The Welshman is illiterate and poor ('ever being chargeable to the Parish'), and he has an uncontrollable temper, as the Highlanders were reputed to have, and indeed foreigners generally (cf. *The Sun*'s comment on Latin tempers in '20 Reasons Why You Should Hate Argies' during the Falklands War). 'Taffy' is compared to the French, enemies of all that is English, and is associated with French rejoicing over the defeat of Marlborough: hence he is a traitor and potential Jacobite (as the verbal echo from anti-Jacobite verse satire also possibly indicates). Moreover, Wales is a ridiculous and irrelevant place, readily characterised under the name of a mock-English county, 'Goatlandshire'. And lest it be thought that this mockery is of little interest given its source in popular culture, it is worthwhile remembering that it is endorsed in historical accounts of Highlandised Jacobitism given by some of the most eminent scholars of the following century (as, for example, in the quotations from Trevelyan cited in the Introduction).⁶

Central to the imperial destiny of Anglo-Britishness celebrated in the confinement of Taffy and his ilk to the fringe was an ethnic justification which rested on the Germanic origins of England, and the predisposition of the Germanic peoples to liberty, which led them to advance (inexorably) towards freedom 'slowly, through blood and tears', as Trevelyan describes this process in the reign of Charles II. From the 'agrarian commonwealth' established by the idealised Saxon king Alfred to the paradise of Whig liberty in the eighteenth century, the Germanic peoples had been dedicated to the pursuit of freedom: so ran the story. Their values, though they could be interfered with (as under the Norman Yoke or James II), were fundamentally unchanging; and England's march to destiny was located in its battle against the grain of such interference to establish the ideal political expression of its ethnicity. The essentially unchanging quality of Germanic liberty was finally victorious over 'Popery and Tyranny' in 1688, and, once this triumph was achieved, Germanic values, constant across *time*, could be extended and incorporated through *space*, by imperialism: hence Seeley's collocation of Highlander and New Zealander as both beneficiaries of the enveloping *Pax Britannica*. Thus when Sir Walter Scott noted that 'an Englishman was not half so much disposed to believe that his ancestors led a very different life from himself' as was a Scot, he was identifying that feature of British rhetoric which, while categorising Scottish medieval history as a 'long brawl' of over-mighty subjects, submerges Bolingbroke's rebellion and the Wars of the Roses in its own consciousness. What is typical of the Scotland which is uncivilised is an aberration in the country which does the civilising: between 1300 and 1603, four English monarchs were assassinated and one died in battle; the figures are two and two for the Scots. But the stasis of the Germanic ideal of liberty across time renders what in non-English history is the fruits of barbarity into (in English history) the intrusive errors of interfering rulers and their sad results. Dynastic war and magnate rivalry are false notes in a symphony of liberty. The popular perception absorbed a rhetoric of imperial Anglo-British origins and destiny, adopted in Scotland after the defeat of both royalist/Jacobite and Presbyterian native historical traditions. It strongly reinforced the sense of a lack of self-worth, as no doubt on some level it was designed to do. The dual idea of the pursuit of liberty's progress through space and stasis in time emphasised the uniqueness of the Germanic experience in England, and any reference to Scotland's own struggles for liberty in the Middle Ages could be conveniently subsumed by citing the Germanic ethnicity of a limited number of Scots. This is stated in extreme form in the Scottish poet John Davidson's lines:

> The Bruce and Wallace wight, I ken,
> Who saved old Scotland from her friends,
> Were mighty northern Englishmen.

Such views were once not uncommon, nor were they always merely metaphorical: Bruce was, in the words of one writer, 'an English baron . . . he would have scorned any connection with the savage kernes of the Highlands, who were never admitted to be Scots'.[7]

In these terms, the Germanic nature of such as Bruce was a guarantee of an ancestral love of liberty which was unfortunately misdirected in their resistance to English civilisation. In the construction of the eighteenth century which arose from the narrative of Germanic liberty as applied to Scotland, the Jacobite risings could be seen as Celtic intrusions into the Germanic Lowlands, an ethnic myth which to some extent persists to this day. Such analyses habitually confuse linguistic and ethnic boundaries: the area of the Gaeltachd, even in the eighteenth century, penetrated into areas which might plausibly be termed 'Lowland', and it was also (embarrassingly) true that the Jacobite risings received very considerable support from the 'Germanic' Lowlands. This was uncomfortable because it suggested the existence of a national rather than merely marginal ethnic/dynastic Jacobitism, with implications for the successful incorporation of Scotland into the spread of Germanic liberties and the glories of British civilisation – and therefore Lowland Jacobitism was largely ignored by history with this particular teleological end in view. As a result of this embritishing, as it may be termed, of Lowland Scotland, the Highlands were increasingly characterised as 'other', and the features which set them apart were more and more strongly delineated. The view of the 'Saxon constitution' as the 'natural state of things' led increasingly to a divorcement between a participating Lowland and non-participatory Highland Scotland. By the 1790s, even radicals like Alexander Aitchison had begun to subscribe to an

Anglocentric model of liberty depending on 'the English constitution so long ago as the days of King Alfred': as Colin Kidd admits, 'English rights acquired by incorporation provided a more convincing platform for Scottish radicalism' than did the homegrown product. Meanwhile, the Highlands were, in Peter Womack's Barthesian phrase, 'colonised by the empire of signs', a colourful place remote from reality, with their inhabitants later to become what have been called 'the indispensable atavistic natives in the Victorian triumph of peace and progress'. Whether as noble savage or plunder-lusting illiterate, the identification of Highlanders with Jacobitism accelerated the pace at which both were pushed to the edges of history. There they were acknowledged only through the conditional nostalgia of Primitivist romanticism, which, since it led to increasing use of land for deer partly in order to create an Ossianic theme park, was hardly an unmixed benefit. By the end of the nineteenth century, 1,700,000 acres of cultivable land in Scotland were under deer. The change from viewing Scotland in its domestic identity (i.e. not as North Britain, but as a distinct cultural zone) as Jacobite to seeing Jacobitism as Highland and not Lowland-Germanic, accomplished in the century which separates the tartans of Culloden from those of Balmoral, provides us with a window on the alliance forged between historical and cultural romanticism to represent Scotland's past in their own terms.[8]

It must be admitted that part of the power achieved by the Myth of the Jacobite Clans was derived from the propaganda of the Jacobite cause itself, primarily through the image of the Highlander as patriot. In the aftermath of the Revolution of 1688–9, it became customary for Jacobitism in Scotland to express its patriotism in Highland terms; this may have had something to do with the 'cult of "tartanry"' which 'briefly flowered in the 1680s' at the royal court, as Michael Lynch tells us. The Highlander was used in Jacobite ideology in an iconic sense, as a symbol of patriotic purity to set against the corruption and bribery associated with the Union from the beginning. The suggestion was not that all Scotland was Highland; rather, it was a matter of personal identification with a national ideal. Hence in James Philp of Almericlose's *Grameid*, an epic poem on Dundee's rising of 1689, Major-General Hugh

Mackay of Scourie is described as the 'Belgic general', though he was a Scot as were many of his soldiers. Despite this, he represents an invading force and an alien ideology, and on this level Highland patriotism symbolises what is most truly native. For example, traditional Scottish songs which told the tale of a Highlander (or gipsy) stealing away a young girl were transformed in the Highlander-as-patriot tradition in groups of songs such as the 'Highland Laddie' cycle, where the young girl represents the unawakened patriotism of Scotland, stirred to life by Jacobite potency:

Will you play me fair play Bonny Ladie Highland Ladie
For another year I'll Stay Bonny Ladie Highland Ladie
For all the Lasses hereabout Bonny Ladie Highland Ladie
Will marry none but Geordie's rout Bonny Ladie Highland Ladie
The time will come when bad choise Bonny Ladie Highland
    Ladie
Will cause them sigh will we rejoice Bonny Ladie Highland
    Ladie,
I'll take you in your Tartan trews Bonny Ladie Highland Ladie,
Before these Rogues that Wear the blues Bonny Ladie Highland
    Ladie.

In some of the songs in this cycle, the girl goes in search of the Highlander, being disappointed by the life offered by 'Lowland Laddies', 'English fops' or 'Butter-Boxes' (Dutchmen: a reference to William's usurpation). When she finds him, he is usually alive with sexual symbolism and heavily armed, the one synecdochally standing for the other, implying his capacity both to renew the land's fertility and to depose the usurper. The girl throws away any trappings of wealth (which symbolise how she has been 'bought and sold for English gold'), and abandons herself to the fruition of sexual glee with her Highland liberator, who in the later stages of this cycle is associated with Charles Edward himself:

He's coming frae the north that's to marry me
He's coming frae the north that's to marry me
A feather in his bonnet, a rose aboon his bree
He's a bonny bonny laddie, an you be he.

The land will have her lover-king again: in some songs, such as 'My Love He Was a Highland Lad', the fertility imagery is explicitly that of a renewed flowering of the nation:

> But there's a bud in fair Scotland,
> A bud weel kend in glamourye;
> And in that bud there is a bloom,
> That yet shall flower o'er kingdoms three;
> And in that bloom there is a brier,
> Shall pierce the heart of tyrannye,
> Or there is neither faith nor truth,
> Nor honour left in our countrye.

From the potentially threatening and disruptive outsider of folk tradition, the Highlander has become a patriotic deliverer (as indeed the very Anglo-Scots of the poetry indicates): and his Highland dress symbolises his patriotism, irrespective of cultural background. In Chapter 2, I will suggest that this was conveniently reflected in the Jacobite leadership's decision to put a large number of its troops, whatever their origin, into Highland dress, a practice found as early as 1689, when 'Mr. Drummond, the advocate' wore 'Highland habit' in Dundee's army.[9]

Charles himself was identified not only as the land's lover and its armed deliverer, but also as the feminised nation herself: hence perhaps the propaganda importance of the 'Betty Burke' episode, and the appearance of Charles in female dress on Jacobite drinking-glasses (admittedly only six of which survive), though this may merely be a way of celebrating his deliverance. Hanoverian propaganda took the episode as an excuse to deride Charles's masculinity; it also seems to have recognised the dangers in the patriotic Highland iconography of Jacobitism, for example by depicting the Prince in the guise of a Highland Pied Piper, come to seduce his immature supporters (rats or children, according to taste) away from their homes and duties.[10]

It is noteworthy that the imagery of Charles as Highland patriot/fertility king was substantially similar in both Highland and Lowland Jacobitism, between which there was frequently little ideological difference. Gaelic poetry portrays the monarchical patriot as a renewer of fertility, while the *aisling* Jacobite poetry of Ireland depicts Ireland herself in much the same role as the 'Highland Laddie' poems, abandoned and seeking deliverance by her true love. Even in England, the idea of a loved and lonely Britannia in Jacobite iconography shows strong similarities: the struggle between Jacobite and Whig over Britannia seems to have been finally resolved about the time of James Thomson's *Rule Britannia* (1740), though the Stuarts had inherited her image as the Virgin Mary and mother of the Church, and had done much to promote her as an icon. In all these cases, the widespread and consistent nature of Jacobite imagery is worth remarking. These were wide margins indeed.[11]

The roots of the historiographical process which led to the sidelining of Jacobitism are significantly located in the competing and prevailing interpretations of the Revolution of 1688. The propagandistic identification of Jacobitism with Catholicism (in fact, the majority of Jacobites were nonjurant Anglicans and Episcopalians – the Catholic Church grew increasingly lukewarm as the century progressed) almost certainly arose in part from the anti-Catholic hysteria surrounding James VII and II. Hysteria in significant part it was: James for example spent less on promoting Catholic education than on the Anglican sacramentalism of the Royal Touch, which Pope Gregory VII had written against. Just as in the case of the Jacobites, there were long-standing suggestions that James's army was packed out with Catholics. Not only has this been disproved by recent research, but it is possible also that William of Orange (of whose invasion the Pope did not disapprove) had as many or more Catholics in his army, as Reresby remarked in 1689. Moreover, James's lenity towards the Quakers and at least partly friendly attitude towards the Huguenots both tended to be marginalised in a historical narrative which emphasised the king's trespasses on Germanic (Protestant) liberty. Saxonicity and the English church had been associated since at least the sixteenth century, while Anglicanism's special place in English society could be allied to Luther's role 'as the most strident defender of the German identity'. The presumed 'historic rights' of the Germanic/Saxon English against 'an innovating crown' combined not with high

Anglicanism's role as the guarantor of the Crown's sacramental jurisdiction, but with the broader Protestant ideal of national autonomy and personal liberty articulated by Luther and some of the more definitively Protestant adherents of the English settlement. While there were exceptions like the Catholic Whig historian Lord Acton, who claimed that the 'Teutonic race received the Catholic ideas wholly and without reserve', it remained the case that 'the Anglo-Saxonism of most of the Protestant historians of the nineteenth century was relatively straightforward'. James VII and II's reign was one of the heartlands of this 'relatively straightforward' approach. In 1988, a best-selling Jacobite historian like Susan Maclean Kybett could still write that 'James's mindset was being fed by a gaggle of Jesuit priests', while other writers speak of 'James . . . and his parasites' and of a king who wanted 'to crush the Anglican Church'. Macaulay long ago described his reign as 'tyranny which approached to insanity', while Trevelyan opined that 'in this persecution [of Nonconformists] James was following the desire of his heart': those who went to France with him were described as having to 'stop and worship idols, while their children were torn from them and educated by priests and nuns'. It is instructive to take a cold look at what traditional English historiography has to say about its kings: in the 1980s *History Today* ran an approbatory review of Richard I, on the cover of which was a picture of the massacre of the Saracen prisoners at Acre, which he organised. The thousands slaughtered by Henry V or Henry VIII affect the traditional verdict of history far less than James's insistence that Magdalen College, Oxford accept a Catholic president, or the Trial of the Seven Bishops. Detaching ourselves from inherited prejudice, it is difficult not to get a sense of the bizarre from such judgements: at least the redoubtably Whig (historically speaking) Dickens condemns virtually all previous monarchs for their barbarity in his *Child's History of England*.[12]

But the key to such accounts lies not in their empirical equity but in the pivotal role played by James's monarchy as the battleground for the final struggle between Germanic liberty's expression through parliamentary sovereignty and the 'Popery and Tyranny' of arbitrary power (Bruce Lenman neatly ironises this by suggesting

that James was among the first to carry out the political centrali-
sation associated with 'libertarian' Thatcherism). Only a handful of
misguided hotheads, tribal warlords, recidivist aristocrats and
criminal elements, the flotsam and jetsam of progress, continued to
support the Stuarts on this reading. Even their motives were mixed,
for only (by implication) a few out-and-out fools wished to see the
Stuarts restored. This differs rather from Christopher Hill's disappointed assessment (shared by Samuel Johnson) that 'manhood
suffrage . . . would have been more likely to lead to a restoration of
the Stuarts than to a just and equal society' in the eighteenth century; but the traditional view is better represented by P. Hume
Brown's opinion that Highland politics was more concerned with
'promoting or opposing the power of the Duke of Argyll than in
concern for the maintenance or the overthrow of the Revolution
settlement'. Even the benighted Highlanders, it seems, must have
favoured or opposed the Jacobites for reasons other than the obvious
ones.[13]

The Scottish Enlightenment period played an important role in
distancing Jacobitism from the mainstream of the historical narrative. In his argument in favour of a Scottish militia in the Seven
Years' War, Alexander Carlyle characterised the '45, then only
fourteen years away, through a projection of national responsibility
onto the Highland 'other'. The country then had been defenceless,
the argument went, against 'five thousand undisciplined militia
from the most remote parts of the kingdom', who had, unopposed,
been allowed to stage a 'pitiful insurrection'. Thus was history
rewritten within the memories of most who had lived through it.
The part played by Edinburgh in 1745, discussed more fully in
Chapter 2, was hidden behind the 'most remote' tartan bogeyman
in order to exculpate Lowland Scotland from the English accusa-
tion of Jacobitism. Scotland could be trusted with a militia, because
it was British.[14]

Carlyle's practical contribution to embritishing was theoretically
paralleled in Lord Kames's *Essay upon British Antiquities* (1747),
which 'accepted the idea of history as progress', while Alexander
Fraser Tytler commented on 'the blessings of a political union'.

This was part of a strongly delineated movement, spurred on by the cleverest men of the day. As Michael Lynch tells us,

> The new philosophical historians, such as David Hume and William Robertson, saw history as the charting of human development through a number of stages, from barbarity to refinement.

Hume himself had been a member of the militia which sought to defend Edinburgh from the Jacobites in 1745: though he attacked English Whig mythology, he did not dissent from the notion of a developing British liberty, which led to an inevitable loosening in the fidelity owed to the specifically Scottish past. In Michael Fry's words, 'it actually felt liberating to close the door on Scotland's dark and cobwebbed past'. In recognition of this changing understanding of history, it is no wonder that the Preface to the *Edinburgh Review* in 1755–6 stated that

> If countries have their ages with respect to improvement, North Britain may be considered as in a state of early youth guided and supported by the more mature strength of her kindred country.

This was almost a statement of Scotland's status as a *tabula rasa*, or at the least a young and impressionable nation to be helped out of its earlier native barbarities: children of the mist indeed, emerging from the mists of time. In such a situation, the country's past might even be viewed as an embarrassment (though this was not always the case). In 1780, for instance, doubts were being raised over the foundation of a society of antiquaries for Scotland, as it might be held to unnecessarily 'call the attention of Scots, to the ancient honours and constitution of their independent monarchy'. The split between a sceptical and romanticised attitude to the past, documented by Marinell Ash, led to a cycle of partisan remythologising, but one which, despite fears of its acting as a catalyst to nationalism, took place in the context of 'a sterile historiography of local colour and romance', like the controversies over both Jacobitism and Mary Queen of Scots. Whether sentimentalised or viewed with a jaundiced eye, both these episodes belonged to the 'old' Scotland, and were its heritage: they had nothing to do with 'new' Britain, or the triumphant march of Whig teleology celebrated in, for example, the novels of Sir Walter Scott. By the time of the Napoleonic wars, fears of a nationalist use for the Scottish past were subsiding in the face of the colourful impotence of its historiography, and Scott contributed to the resulting cultus of redundant history to a great degree. Among older historical episodes, the stories of loyal Bruce and Wallace, which the Jacobites had adopted in the eighteenth century for patriotic purposes, could in the nineteenth either become sentimentalised into a similar marginality or be part of Germanic Scotland's misdirected search for liberty, later fulfilled in Union. The Presbyterians tended to be happier with post-Reformation history in any case. After the Disruption,

> the two competing churches took over respective slices of the Scottish past to buttress their claims to historicity – and, at the same time, were content to leave the Middle Ages, which they regarded as a time of popery and darkness, to the Catholics and Episcopalians.

Thus the stories of Bruce and Wallace became the account of a 'redundant state of society', combined either with romantic remoteness or misplaced Germanicity, in either event veiled in the mists of popery and prelacy. In this way, it was domestic religious patriotism which helped to confirm the appropriateness and power of an incorporating narrative of British events.[15]

As the eighteenth century progressed, the teleology of English constitutionalism was increasingly accepted. Scotland's past became recategorised as a three-stage caricature. First came the 'long brawl' of medieval warfare between over-mighty magnates. In this context, 'the negative associations of magnate anarchy and feudal oppression' joined forces with native sectarianism to undermine appreciation of what was arguably the period of the apogee of independent Scottish achievement. The second stage was the dark night of religious fanaticism and civil war, which could be given an interesting patriotic gloss as Presbyterian resistance to English Stuart oppression. As the Stuarts were emblematic of anti-constitutionalism, popery, tyranny and arbitrary power in Whig eyes, this 'patriotism' did not ultimately tend to compromise Anglo-Scottish relations. The third stage was the 'burying of national pretensions', when the Scots became mature enough to realize that they were 'bankrupt' and 'had only a set of discredited institutions and a debunked ancient constitution in their historical treasury'. In this context, 'it was the new dawn of Union and Anglicisation which had dispelled the nightmare of Scottish feudal oppression and backwardness'. Scotland had at last grown up.[16]

The 'refinement' sought by many in eighteenth-century Scottish society was a 'product of modernity' in these terms, and involved a reining-in of 'primitivist instincts'. These included the idea which I outlined in *The Invention of Scotland*, that Scottish history was the history of liberty and struggles for liberty against England. Such a view could have no place in the Anglo-British Germanic narrative of the development of national (i.e. British) liberty from the days of authentic Saxon custom to the triumph of the Whig constitution; instead it must be excluded from the story. Insofar as Jacobitism was an (embarrassingly recent) component of Scottish history as liberty, it was necessary to marginalise it: hence Lowland Scots wishing to take advantage of the benefits of the new Britain strongly dissociated themselves and their community from Jacobitism from the 1750s onwards (though once it was finally defeated, they might reassociate themselves with a Highlandised version of it, suitably glossed with romantic sentiment). This in its turn reinforced the notion of the 1745 Rising as Highland, even though in the very year that David Hume published *The Enquiry Concerning Human Understanding* (1748) there were Jacobite mobs on the High Street and the Canongate in Edinburgh. Lowland Jacobitism was, as we shall see, a powerful force: but it was in the interests of the developing British identity to push it to one side, for 'North Britishness was a Scottish version of English whig identity, based on a commitment to English constitutional history'.[17]

But there was also another factor confining Jacobitism to 'the narrowing world of the Highlands'. This was the development of primitivism, whether in the guise espoused by Smollett, that the English were 'too corrupted by luxury to support the British

Empire' and needed Celtic savages to help them out (as was evident from the Seven Years' War casualty figures), or in the literary triumphs of James Macpherson. The central function of primitivism relating to Scotland was to glamorise the Highland way of life while decontextualising its achievements. The separateness of the Highlands was a guarantee of their otherness, as indeed might be the special qualities of the landscape itself: Womack has called sublimity (the cult of the sublime, virtually contemporaneous with primitivism) the mark 'of the political subjection of the Gaeltacht'. The Highlands were the playground of primary epic, a historyless zone which was only historicised by sale in the market to a ready audience who could admire the heritage of sturdy primitives while knowing that they posed no threat. In this way, the image of the Highlander as patriot was taken advantage of, both for British Army recruitment purposes, and also in the development of an illusion of primitive nobility, untouched by the realities of historical change.[18]

James Macpherson had a crucial, if ambivalent, role in this process. He was born into the divided and uneasy country which was Scotland in 1736/8. Despite a recent suggestion that he was 'a sophisticated and latitudinarian Scottish whig', Macpherson's background was deeply rooted in two kinds of Jacobite society: the clan country of his background and boyhood, and the Scoto-Latin inheritance of King's College, Aberdeen. Born in Kingussie and brought up in Badenoch, Macpherson as a boy witnessed both General Cope's advance against the Prince's army and Major-General Gordon's attack on Ruthven barracks. At the 1745 Rising's end, Macpherson may have joined his cousin in 'hurling stones at the troops who were setting fire to the Chief's house'. In his early poetry, such as 'The Hunter' or 'On the Death of Marshal Keith', Macpherson uses Jacobite metaphors and topoi in subject-matter charged with wish-fulfilment and regret. The latter was to predominate in an Ossian cycle which acted as a

> dirge for the ancient civilisation which in his own day and in his own strath he saw dominated and depressed by the coarse, dull emissaries of the raw materialistic civilisation of the south.[19]

Macpherson's Ossian cycle (*Fragments of Ancient Poetry Collected in the Highlands*, *Fingal* and *Temora* all came out in the early 1760s) portrays a heroic world over which the shadows of sadness and regret seem perpetually to linger. As I have argued elsewhere, in much of this recasting of oral material, Macpherson is giving a coded lament for the defeat of Stuart hopes, as he had in his earlier elegy for Marshal Keith, where the Keiths, 'relics of a dying race', are 'lost to all but fame, / And only living in the hero's name', their halls 'decayed' places where 'with each gust of wind a fragment falls'. A similar enervated landscape pervades the Ossian poetry.[20]

Despite John Pinkerton's denunciation of Ossianic patriotism as 'the last effort of Celticism to injure the history of Britain' (if this was the case, its primitivism found little echo in Irish cultural nationalism, as Clare O'Halloran has pointed out), Macpherson's 'dirge' can be read as a distancing of his subject from history through sentiment. Macphersonian landscape is vacant and ruined into sublimity as surely as the heroism of its characters is extinguished in pathos. The loss continues, the victories of the past pass away: what that past provides is a sublimating elegy for Jacobite history, moving it into the historyless zone of primary epic. The songs are over, the times are finished: heroic Celticism is iconised, and its iconographer detaches it from the narrative of human history and its continuing agenda. In this sense, Macpherson is abetting an account of the past which marginalises the very subject that he claims for the centrepiece of his epic.[21]

Yet such a critique of Ossian's role ignores the fact that Macpherson has proved no comfortable figure to canonical British history and criticism. His achievement, despite the fact that it rests to a considerable degree on Gaelic sources, has been repeatedly disparaged as forgery (by an interesting twist, which may raise questions about attitudes to Gaelic culture in general, Burns is praised for dressing up oral material, while Macpherson is attacked for it). While the undisputed English forger Chatterton has largely retained the cultural image of the 'marvellous Boy', perhaps because of his tragic early death, Macpherson has continued to suffer greater hostility. In the context of his achievement, truly remarkable comments are still available from distinguished historians. In 1983, Hugh Trevor-Roper suggested that Macpherson was a forger who transplanted Irish myth into Scotland (Lord Dacre was obviously forgetful of the Ossianic folklore of Glen Lyon, only one *locus amoenus* for the story); while in 1992, Linda Colley made the quite extraordinary suggestion, in her acclaimed book *Britons*, that Macpherson '*invented* the romantic Celtic hero Ossian' (my italics). Macpherson is thus rendered not only a forger but also a fantasist, with his part in a Highland 'invention of tradition' a fraudulent apologia for a lack of origins in comparison with those of Anglo-Britain. In this sense, it is clear that Macpherson's epic, on one level reducible to anodyne heritage, on another touched a raw cultural nerve. There is something uncomfortable about Ossian, despite its separation of the Highlands from continuing history. Perhaps John Pinkerton was not so far from the truth: by leaving the Jacobite elements in his work emplaced in code, Macpherson not only gives them a shadowy energy which provides useful raw material for the primitivist dimension of Romanticism, the sublimity of Wordsworth's 'old, unhappy far-off things, and battles long ago': Macpherson also ennobles, albeit on his terms, the marginalised Gaeltachd. 'At the height of the Scottish Enlightenment, Scotland was presented as an anti-Enlightenment culture, to the delight of all Europe', while Macpherson's 'patriotic view that the Irish Ossianic ballads were ultimately derived from Scotland' served only to underline the cultural nationalism of an enterprise which, while it detached Celtic Scotland from history, confirmed its heroic qualities at a time when these were still tainted by Jacobitism. Macpherson's 'forging' was a metonymy of transcendence: Ossian's Fianna were encoded Jacobites, and the Fianna were victorious, as Fergus's Scots had been in 'The Hunter', that early Macpherson poem; but, as in 'The Hunter', the knowledge of what really happened (the defeat of the cause) is present as foreboding or loss. Such foreboding or loss is the price of romance; and in the sense that the Ossian poems are romance, they too served their turn in distancing the past into sentiment. But to the extent that that romance was animated by a real expression not just of nostalgia but also of regret, Macpherson's epic offered a disturbing hint of injustice lingering amid its sentimental treatment of grief and loss. This is an ambivalence which Macpherson shares with Scott; but the former leaves it inconclusive, while the latter closes his narrative with a victory for Whig history and subscribes to a Germanic characterisation of Lowland Scotland which Macpherson rejected. It has been argued that this rejection was not always a consistent one; but the key here is surely the preface to *Fingal*, with its assertion of the Celticism of Caledonia as against the 'German' identity with which it was labelled by Tacitus. As I have argued elsewhere, 'the identification of Scotland as entirely Celtic was almost always [in the hands of those sympathetic to Jacobitism] one which sought to minimise divisions between Highland and Lowland in the interests of patriotic unity'.[22]

In some respects, then, the Ossian poems are the end of an old song; in others, their ostensible primitivism speaks to issues still active in their contemporary Scottish society. Wordsworth's 'Solitary Reaper' is more truly a sentimental projection of identity than anything by Macpherson: the girl whom the English poet cannot understand may, far from mourning 'battles long ago', be singing of the contemporary injustice of the Clearances under the guise of a traditional model. Macpherson was after all a Gael, and used Gaelic 'to convey any confidential information'. Hence his creation of heritage and great gift to primitivism carries about it shades of national and nationalist ambiguity, more so than in the general run of the cult of Highland primitivism, which alternated 'the figures of fool, rogue and beggar' with the 'numinous value of relics'. The increasing collection of oral culture which followed Ossian was often (though there were many exceptions) associated with a confirmation of the declining and marginal status of those who practised it. Oral culture's strong links to Jacobite culture, ideology and historiography (cf. Sir George Mackenzie's reliance on '*Oral Tradition*' and the 'probable Tradition' of the past in his defence of Stuart claims) may to some extent have tied the romanticisation of Jacobitism to the primitivist interest in the oral. While Whig history iconised documents such as Magna Carta, its teleology was also rooted in little more than a vague foundation myth with a small popular tradition behind it. This did not prevent its ascendancy,

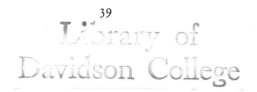

while that culture associated with Jacobite ideology was being collected and converted from oral discontent to the documentation of an historical era forever departed – was in fact being rendered a document of Whig sentimentality.[23]

Several writers have doubted the link between Jacobitism and oral culture, usually by claiming that the Jacobite song (for example) was not contemporary with the events which it describes – or that if it was, it was a piece of private gentry writing, unconnected to oral culture. As so often in discussion of Jacobitism, this merely remythologises what it sets out to demythologise. Just as in the case of Jacobite recruitment, empirical evidence is bursting to be attended to, but is often ignored. Jacobite material was indeed apparently not transmitted *purely* orally very often (though this must be a provisional judgement); but the 'purely oral' in the eighteenth century is a doubtful category in a literate culture, even one with only modest communications. There is, however, large-scale evidence for balladeering and widespread dissemination of Jacobite writing, both in peacetime and among those who carried arms for the Stuarts, which has been adduced at length elsewhere: such songs seem to have been frequently transmitted orally. Undoubtedly, many sentimental Jacobite songs were composed in the Romantic period and afterwards: there was a demand for them, as it was not until well into the nineteenth century that the unbowdlerised lyrics of aggressive Jacobitism seem to have become respectable. Indeed, the process of collecting eighteenth-century Jacobite song created (as probably was the case with the ballads) a heritage text, which excluded some aspects of the tradition and sentimentalised others. The development of nostalgia for the impossibly remote is part both of Romanticism and the picturesque fascination with the Highlands which reached its apogee in the Victorian period.[24]

Such sentimentality was not without its dangers. The appropriation of the Jacobite Highlander as patriotic icon for government recruiting purposes served to provide a limited integration for these Celtic primitives in the British Army (where their casualty rate in the Seven Years' War was 32 per cent as against the Anglo-American figure of 9 per cent: they might as well have been at Culloden). As Bruce Lenman says, the avowed objective [of recruiting] was to transport potential Jacobites to foreign battlefields where they could be slaughtered fighting the French, rather than leave them to plot subversion at home.

Moreover, such practice, as well as sending men abroad, also detached officially recognised Highland values from contemporary issues such as the Clearances. If the romanticised Highlands belonged to the past, what was happening to them in the present lost its force: the focus was on a world remote from contemporaneity, though concerned individuals like Colonel Stewart of Garth tried to bring the traditions up to date. Sentimentality towards the Highlands was an ideal partner for heritage: a possessed past admired because its distance lends enchantment to the view. Hence perhaps a chief like MacDonell of Glengarry, arrayed in an intense display of finery, might be among the foremost clearers. Whig history has taught its readers that it is not worth sentimentalising because it is invincible, while it takes care to depict the Jacobite cause labouring under the sweet aura of inevitable defeat. 'We wuz robbed' is a phrase infinite in possibility, absent in performance. Insofar as some of the ideological motivations behind Jacobitism are still of living concern, it is necessary for heritage to camouflage what cannot be distanced. The Myth of the Jacobite Clans helps to underline the marginalisation of Jacobitism which is central to a denial of its relevance.[25]

The burden of this chapter is thus that the details underlying the misrepresentation of the Jacobite cause, particularly the '45, have all in different ways served to reinforce a view which is partial and inadequate. That this is not always the case must be freely admitted in doing justice to the work of many fine historians; but that it is nonetheless frequently so, is sadly not to be doubted. The prevalence of the romantic/sceptic dichotomy regarding 1745 is still a marked one, even though we have now reached the 250th anniversary of the events of the Year of the Prince. The equation of Scots with Jacobites gave way to the characterisation of Jacobites as Highlanders and Scots (for military purposes) as Highlanders too, though doubtless commercial, civic and Germanic enough in roles more suited to the internal development of British society. We still reside to a degree in the confusion caused by this inconsistent and inaccurate cultural modelling. In Chapter 2, I intend to show in detail the nature and extent of Jacobite support in the major risings, particularly the '45, which exerts a fascination almost directly proportionate to the lack of accuracy with which it is (all too frequently) portrayed. The substance and motivation of Lowland Jacobite support has been admitted before; it is demonstrated in detail in the pages that follow, addressed to the Myth of the Jacobite Clans.

CHAPTER 2

The Myth of the Jacobite Clans

The Jacobites certainly regarded the Union as a major political gift to them, for it handed them the leadership of nationalist sentiment in Scotland . . . old Presbyterian nationalism . . . was a dead cause after 1707.

Bruce Lenman

Because Lowland support was not . . . negligible in amount, the Jacobite army of 1745 was able to avoid some of the disasters that had previously faced similar forces.

Jean McCann

The lairds and bailies of the Lowlands . . . had done their best to ignore Charles Edward.

Christopher Harvie[1]

John Graham of Claverhouse, Viscount Dundee, left Edinburgh with fifty horse at the beginning of the spring of 1689, as the Convention of Estates declared for King William. Between then and his raising the royal standard on Dundee Law on 16 April, a month later, King James's lieutenant-general acquired little in the way of additional support. So began the Jacobite saga, and Dundee, like Montrose a Lowland cavalier, held command over what was essentially a Highland army, leaving aside the battalion of Irish troops commanded by Colonel (later Major-General) Cannon (the Earl of Melfort had promised Dundee more than 5000 Irish troops, but relatively few of these actually arrived). Although quite a number of the Lowland gentry were thought to be sympathetic, few were actually with Dundee's force. 'The loyall shires of Banf, Aberdeen, Merns, Angus, Pearth, and Stirling' contrived to furnish many fewer troops than they were to do in subsequent risings. Thus at the time of Killiecrankie, Dundee found himself almost entirely reliant on the western clans: Glengarry, MacDonald of Sleat, Stewart of Appin, Sir John Macleod, MacDonald of Keppoch, MacDonald of Glencoe, Clanranald and Lochiel, and Sir Alexander Maclean. Farquharson of Inverey and a few Lowland cavalry and gentry were the only exceptions to this rule among the Scots. The Highlanders seem to have prided themselves on their traditional way of fighting, believing (according to Lochiel's *Memoirs*) that theirs was the ancestral Scottish way: other Scots 'have never made such a figure in the field since they gave over these [Highland] weapons', and were thus by implication degenerate from their ancestors.[2]

Killiecrankie itself was a battle contested by tiny forces. Dundee had barely 2000, and Major-General Mackay not many more. Yet it was a very costly one for both sides, suffering half as many casualties again as did the Boyne with fewer than a tenth of the combatants: almost half of those who fought were killed. Although the Highlanders were on their natural territory and charged downhill, and although Mackay's troops suffered what became well-publicised difficulties with their plug bayonets, the battle foreshadowed Culloden more than is usually credited. Apart from Dundee's own death, 30 per cent of the Jacobite force fell in a frontal attack against Mackay's musketry: the casualties were proportionately higher than in the later battle. With level ground, strong artillery and the flanking action of the Argyll militia (as occurred in 1746), the Williamite general would have won the day. Only the accession of forces to the Jacobites after Killiecrankie disguised the Pyrrhic nature of the victory (though, Dundee being dead, the numbers who joined fell far short of Mackay's fear that 'the whole north' would declare for Claverhouse if he won a victory). Of course, Cannon and Buchan's attempts soon petered out in failure, though the former retained an army large enough to harry the Lowlands until a few months after the defeat at Cromdale in 1690. Eventually, as the Jacobite force split up into smaller groups, it ceased to be effective, and the last Scottish Jacobite outposts had surrendered by 1692.[3]

Dundee's army, largely like Montrose's, was a small fast-moving force, more akin to the royalist units of the Civil War period than the Jacobite forces which followed it. It was not well suited to holding territory, electing local magistrates, stable Lowland recruiting and similar duties; nor is there much evidence that Dundee could have successfully faced a regular army of 10,000, as the Jacobites did at Falkirk in 1746, their concentrated firepower surprising Hawley's expectations. Victories outwith the Highlands were hard to come by for forces such as Dundee's, except under superior generalship: yet in 1745–6 the Jacobite army prevailed in four engagements, suffering its only defeat behind the Highland line. As this chapter will demonstrate, the armies raised to fight for the Stuarts in 1715 and 1745 came much closer in strength to national precedents for full Scottish mobilisation than did the small and overwhelmingly Highland force of 1689.[4]

It may seem strange that in a book directed at exposing the myth of the Highland nature of the Jacobite forces, I should begin with the admission that the force of 1689 largely fits this description. But the point of the argument is not to deny that there was extensive Highland support for the Jacobites: that would be folly, and this chapter will provide evidence for Highland as well as Lowland recruitment. I seek rather to explain the presence and falsity of the myth of an almost ubiquitously Highland Jacobitism, particularly as it affects the Rising of 1745. The crucial element in the need to explain Jacobitism in these terms is found in the manner in which Scotland was incorporated into British history in the eighteenth century. The single event which of course did more than any other to incorporate Scotland in that history is Union. The irony may be that it was the Union which guaranteed the Jacobites significant Lowland support: at the time of its passing, 'two-thirds of Scotland were Stuart in sympathy', while 'even supporters of the Union admitted that more than three-quarters of the Scottish people disliked it'.[5]

Although it is possible to trace the heartlands of Jacobite support back to the behaviour of the 'conservative north' of Scotland in the Covenanting period (for example, by the end of May 1638, the only places where the Covenant had not been widely signed were the West Highlands north of Argyll, Aberdeenshire and Banffshire), the forces raised by Montrose and Dundee very seldom exceeded 5000 men. The Covenanters could rely on four times as many, and royalist forces were often even smaller: the 2000 under Lord Aboyne and Sir George Ogilvie of Banff who resisted the National Covenant in the north at the end of the 1630s were not untypical. By contrast, the armies raised in the major post-Union Jacobite risings were several times this size. It was in particular 'after the Act of Union' that 'Jacobites operated as a clearly identifiable group within the framework of the Scottish political system'. This was also true within the British Parliament, since 'throughout the 1710 elections the Scots Jacobite Tories showed all the characteristics of a contemporary political party', and it was their aim 'to do something effectually for the King [James], and by restoring him dissolve the Union'. According to Daniel Szechi, sixteen seats of the forty-five in Scotland went to their candidates. Among them were such men as Sir Alexander Erskine, Lord Lyon King at Arms and MP for Fife; William Livingstone, MP for Aberdeen Burghs (probably a Jacobite); Lord James Murray, MP for Perthshire; the Hon. James Murray (a future Secretary of State to King James), MP for Dumfriesshire; General Charles Ross of Balnagowan, MP for Ross; and John Carnegie of Boysack, MP for Forfarshire, who was out in 1715. This group achieved at least one of their aims in the role they played in gaining qualified toleration for the Episcopalian confession in 1712.[6]

The Episcopalian church's role in Lowland Jacobitism, widely acknowledged, was indeed central. Presbyterianism in Scotland only held the allegiance of a secure majority south of the Tay, and more than half the population lived north of it. From the days of Erskine of Dun, Superintendent (Bishop) of Angus and Mearns from 1562 to 1589, and 'sole representative of the burgesses of Scotland at the wedding of Mary Queen of Scots to the Dauphin of France', through the resistance of the Aberdeen Doctors to the Covenant in the 1630s, the east coast had been sympathetic to Episcopacy. As Gordon Donaldson notes, of those who were deprived for failing to accept the 1662 Episcopal settlement, 75 per cent came from south of the Forth, while in 1690 only four of 200 clergy in the synods of Aberdeen, Banff, Moray, Ross and Caithness 'conformed to Presbyterianism'. In this they were at one with Erskine's 1572 statement, that 'to take away the office of bishop were to take away the order which God hath appointed in His Kirk'.[7]

An examination of the 1708 synod figures by Jean McCann in her 1963 thesis on Jacobite support bears out the above figures. The lists suggest (accepting a pro-Episcopalian bias in parish vacancies, 'often the result of a continued refusal by the congregation to accept a non-Episcopal cleric') that Moray and Ross were more than 50 per cent Episcopalian, Caithness, Aberdeenshire, Angus and Mearns 40–50 per cent, Perthshire and Stirling about 20 per cent, and everywhere else where the church significantly survived was in the 10–15 per cent range – and this was nearly twenty years after disestablishment. If these figures are accurate (and for the sake of argument equalising the size of parishes), they indicate around 250,000–300,000 Episcopalians in Scotland at the time of the Union, with close to a preponderance north of the Tay. With the exception of Caithness (for which there are local factors), every Episcopal area was also Jacobite. This link was fully and finally recognised in the penal legislation of 1746, which enacted that Scottish Episcopal holy orders were invalid, and capped this attack on the church by prescribing that *'no Scottish Priest, whether he took the Oaths or not, was to be allowed to officiate'*. Episcopal ideology was regarded as a serious danger. As John Gibson says:

> Deposed bishops of the Church of Scotland, and the episcopalian-minded nobility and gentry of the north-east remained staunch for King James' indefeasible hereditary right to the Scottish Crown, however much English prelates and magnates had subverted their own consciences.

Whether or not this overstates the case, there was little doubt that the Episcopal element was central to Jacobite culture and support. Moreover, both in parts of the Highlands and in the northern Lowlands, it found itself in tacit alliance with Catholicism:

> the Popish lords naturally threw their weight in with the prelatic party . . . who were far more likely to tolerate their presence than the Presbyterians. As the King also had allied himself with this party . . . the Popish lords and their descendants developed into the staunchest supporters of the monarchy.

Catholicism remained strong in the north-east. Something of the order of 200 were confirmed in a single day in 1706 according to the report of the Presbytery of Kincardine O'Neil, and at least one writer has opined that the magistrates of Montrose were willing to re-embrace Catholicism in the 1680s. In Aberdeen itself, the painted ceiling in the chapel at Provost Skene's house designed for its subsequently Covenanting owner in the 1620s showed (particularly in the depiction of the coronation of the Blessed Virgin Mary as Queen of Heaven) the continuing power of Catholic imagery. The penalties for popery in Scotland were evaded most at the beginning of the eighteenth century in Buchan, Deeside and Strathbogie, all areas with large Episcopalian populations, whose own suspected status may well have served to mute any anti-Catholicism. Moreover, Bourignonism and the religious ideas associated with Madame Guyon spread ecumenically through both denominations in the north-eastern Lowlands. It was small wonder that in a part of the country where Episcopal lairds might have more time for the Archbishop of Cambrai (Fenelon) than for that of Canterbury, Catholicism should prosper in a limited fashion. Bishop Nicholson, Scotland's first Catholic prelate since the Union of the Crowns, was, like his Episcopal counterparts, associated with Jacobite plots and support. The denominations could even appear allied: for example, the 'Memoirs of the Rebellion in 1745 and 1746, so far as it concerned the counties of Aberdeen and Banff' records that 'a very great and good understanding there was betwixt the Nonjurants and them [Catholics], so that Seaton, a

priest, and Law, a Nonjurant minister, were very commonly joined
together among Lord Lewis Gordon's council'. In the Highlands,
Jean McCann remarks, Episcopalians and Roman Catholics were
'closely mingled' in Ardnamurchan and the Cameron country: 'the
Episcopalian Lochiel had a Jesuit brother' (although this was
apparently a matter which gave rise to some dispute in the family).
In northern Scotland, the Catholics were able to open seminaries:
the first at Loch Morar in 1714, then one at Scalan in Glenlivet
three years later.[8]

At the accession of George I, the Episcopalians attacked his
Lutheranism, which was acceptable neither to the low church
(because of its trappings and church decoration) nor, it seems, to
the high (because of George's rejection of caesaro-sacramentalist
symbolism such as the Royal Touch). Such attacks combined with
adverse attitudes towards the Union to make the Episcopalian
heartland a fertile recruiting ground for Mar's Rising of 1715. Many
of Mar's army were Lowlanders, and, in keeping with their leader's
power base, there was a markedly east-coast bias to Jacobite activity. As Michael Lynch says, 'The '15 was never quite the Highland
rising which the government, once it was over, chose to portray it
as. The core of its active support had been in the north-eastern
shires of Aberdeen, Forfar, Kincardine and Angus'. The pattern of
declarations of James's authority matched this profile. On 20
September, the Earl Marischal proclaimed James at Aberdeen, and
raised Aberdeen and Kincardineshire; the Marquis of Huntly
proclaimed the king at Gordon Castle, with Lord Panmure at
Brechin and Lords Ogilvy and Dundee at Dundee, raising Forfarshire, while the Earl of Southesk proclaimed James at Montrose.
Sir Peter Frazer of Durris expressed Hanoverian concerns to the
Lord Justice Clerk thus: 'the situation of his Majesty's friends and
servants is in a very bad condition in this part of Britain . . . We hear
of nothing but distributing Commissions, receiving of arms and
Linnen cloaths making for the Regiments'.[9] Among the Lowland
nobles who rallied to Mar were the marquesses of Huntly,
Tullibardine and Drummond, and Earls Marischal, Murray,
Nithsdale, Wintoun, Erroll, Aboyne, Traquair, Southesk, Home,
Perth, Wigtown, Strathmore, Breadalbane, Carnwath, Dunfermline,

Panmure and Linlithgow (as well as the Earl of Seaforth from the Highland nobility). Viscounts and barons who rose included Kilsyth, Dundee, Kenmure, Frendraught, Kingston, Kintore, Stormont, Rollo, Duffus, Drummond, Strathallan, Inverurie, Inverness, Nairne, Ogilvie, Fraser, Sempill and Forbes of Pitsligo. Patten's list of magnate sympathies lists a potential maximum of 49,720 troops, 39,500 Lowland and 10,220 Highland, of whom up to 34,400 may have been Jacobites (incidentally, Lowland and Highland magnates alike are listed as 'chiefs'). Such figures suggest that up to over two-thirds of the available forces in Scotland could be expected to show Jacobite leanings. It is not, however, a measure of the numbers which could practicably be raised.[10]

By October 1715, Mar had gathered over 900 cavalry and eight infantry battalions (2700 men) from the Lowlands (at the beginning of October, clan figures were 2435). On Sunday 9 October, there were 10,666 Jacobite foot and 1617 horse. By late October there were thousands more: one government estimate suggested that out of 17,700 under arms, only 4100 (23 per cent) were clansmen (though this is almost certainly an underestimate). Eventually, Mar's total forces reached 20,000 men, 12,000–20,000 at the lowest estimate (the Taylers suggest up to 20,000, Rae 12,600 at the beginning of October and 16,700 before Sheriffmuir, Sinclair-Stevenson 12,000 at the beginning of November, Szechi 12,000–20,000). By late in the year, Mar had forty-six battalions under his command (which a government spy, after enumerating, adds up incorrectly!). Mar's army probably peaked before Sheriffmuir: at the time of the battle there were under 9000 effectives available in Scotland (the Anglo-Scottish army defeated at Preston had reached about 3700, and Mar had suffered desertions in Scotland before Sherriffmuir). Whatever the fluctuations, however, the force raised in 1715 was, as will be shown, one which bore comparison with other armies raised in early modern Scotland.[11]

Within this host, the strength of Lowland Jacobitism was clear, although it is difficult to be precise about the relative numbers of Highlanders and Lowlanders in Mar's army; however, good guesswork is possible. The government list of forty-six battalions (including seventeen Lowland and mixed) does not give a complete account of Mar's forces, nor does the list made at Perth on 5 November 1715. This latter does, however, give a more detailed apportionment of strength between Lowland and Highland forces. The cavalry is counted at twenty-one troops (all but one Lowland, though Huntly's horse is borderline). Of the infantry, there are four battalions brigaded under Huntly, of which three are Lowland; three primarily Lowland battalions under Tullibardine; five Highland battalions brigaded under Seaforth; and another nine battalions almost equally divided, with a slight Highland bias. In addition, there are eleven Highland battalions listed at Auchterarder or as not yet having joined the main force, and some troops north of the Forth. Taken together, these roughly suggest that ten out of thirty-two infantry battalions are Lowland, as are 90 per cent of the cavalry: perhaps 4300 out of a 10,200 total in this list, amounting to 42 per cent overall. This figure is well matched in the numbers for the review at Auchterarder before Sheriffmuir, with about 3900 from 8800 being in mainly Lowland units, or 44 per cent. Of Brigadier Mackintosh's initial command in his southern foray, 1150 from 2000 were mainly Lowland units, and with the accession of 600 cavalry in five troops under Viscount Kenmure at Kelso on 24 October, this became 1750 from 2600. Given that Huntly's initial force of northern infantry was between 1400 and 2000 rather than the 800 which appeared at Auchterarder (even accepting that he had Highlanders among his cavalry – the 'light horse'), it appears reasonable to suggest that half or just over half the total force was Lowland. Given the presence of 1100 Englishmen, the Highlanders were (as in 1745) in a minority in Mar's army. In 1745, Lowland troops were as likely to be found in their localities as in the field; if this was also the case in 1715, the proportion of Lowland troops would rise still further. On the other hand, the overall figure can also be modified by the likelihood of a number of mixed units. The uniforming of Lowland troops in Highland dress, discussed above, was a practice which we know took place in the three risings of 1689, 1715 and 1745. In 1715, Lord Drummond 'endeavoured to pass all upon the world as Highlanders' who had enlisted in his three battalions, while Lord Panmure's battalion was one-third Highland.[12]

Whatever the exact figures, there was certainly very strong Jacobite support outside the Highlands. In Aberdeen, Jacobite magistrates were freely elected: as late as 1832, Alexander Bannerman described the election of his Jacobite ancestor Patrick as '*by his fellow citizens*', not '*by the self-elected corporation*'. There was a total of ninety-four Jacobite burgesses in Aberdeen, and in rural Aberdeen and Banffshire Church of Scotland presbyteries 'could not safely meet'. The poorer people in Aberdeen seemed to favour the Stuarts, as did the gentry in the countryside. Angus and Mearns had been regarded as strong for the Jacobites by Captain Ogilvie in his work as *agent provocateur* for Harley, and they fulfilled this opinion in 1715 (and in 1745). There was popular Jacobite celebration on the streets, including the fiddle tunes which were the ubiquitous sign of Jacobite folk culture in Scotland. The lack of seditious words gave no grounds for prosecution, but there was little doubt that the air carried its message to the listeners. An occasion of this kind is no doubt recalled in 'The Piper of Dundee':

> He play'd 'The Welcome owre the Main',
> And, 'Ye'se be fou and I'se be fain',
> And 'Auld Stuarts back again',
>   Wi' muckle mirth and glee . . .

> He play'd 'The Kirk', he played 'The Queer',
> 'The Mullin Dhu' and 'Chevalier' . . .
> And wisnae he a roguie,
> A roguie, a roguie,
> And wisnae he a roguie,
>   The Piper o' Dundee ?

In Dundee itself, the magistrates favoured King James, though there was pro-Hanoverian feeling in the town. In Perthshire, 'the country people flocked to see him; and, as he rode slowly, they pressed forward to touch him, his horse, or any part of its furniture they could reach'. Further north, a troop of horse was raised from Elgin alone, while the strength of Jacobite feeling in Banff and Moray even after the 1715 Rising is attested in an intelligence report to the Lord Justice Clerk. The sixteen Banff and Aberdeenshire lairds who surrendered at Banff in March 1716 were 'dealt with in a very lenient spirit'; the Justice of the Peace system in Scotland was riddled with Jacobitism, as recent research has shown:

> In August and September 1715, 261 JPs (almost one in five) were dismissed for suspected Jacobite sympathies and 198 new appointments made. If this was a purge it was far from comprehensive, as events would prove; after the rising 77 per cent of the JPs in Kincardine were dismissed, 54 per cent of those in Forfarshire, a half of those in Inverness-shire, and three in ten of those in Aberdeenshire. The extent of the disaffection from the Hanoverian regime in 1714–15 was almost incalculable . . . (Lynch, 1991, 327)

As Elizabeth Carmichael has argued, the JP system enabled Jacobites to 'operate' 'as a clearly identifiable group within the framework of the Scottish political system' 'for almost fifty years after the Act of Union'. When James landed in what he called 'my own ancient kingdom' at Peterhead, he found at least the northern part of it secure for him. Argyll wrote to Townshend on 24 September 1715 that: 'On the other side of this river [Forth], excepting our few friends in the North and those of my vassals in the West Highlands, they have a hundred to one at least in their interest'. Pardonable exaggeration in the face of difficult odds or not, Argyll is bearing witness to an essential truth about the strength of Mar's army and its sympathisers which would continue to be significantly borne out in the forces raised by Charles Edward thirty years later.[13]

In the interim, both government and Jacobite agents remained nervous and watchful. The nervousness of the authorities was manifested in, for example, the shooting in Edinburgh on 10 June 1721 (James's birthday), recorded by Lockhart of Carnwath. On this occasion 'a parcell of boys . . . gott together, having whyte roses in their hats, near the Netherbow'. The Canongate guard opened fire, killing a man and a woman who were bystanders: 'Tho this was . . . contrary to all law, we are not to expect any redress'. It was the development of a climate such as this, amplified by the such events as the riots against the malt tax in 1725, which helped to cultivate the unruly urban mood that finally and devastatingly gave vent in the Porteous Riots of 1736. Lowland disaffection was barely touched by the failure of the brief and almost completely Highland rising of 1719. By the 1740s, Jacobite activity was intensifying once more, spurred on by the unpopularity of the government and the plots of Murray of Broughton and his allies.[14]

Lowland support is more often conceded to the Rising of 1715 than to that of 1745, which is sometimes characterised as having been returned to the marginality of Dundee's attempt: 'The rising which broke out after the landing of Prince Charles Edward Stewart . . . was, unlike the abortive attempts in 1708 and 1715, a Highland affair from its beginning to the end thirteen months later' (Lynch, 1991, 334). Even when the facts compromise it, there are those who have been reluctant to concede that the Year of the Prince was not a clan-based struggle sourced in the Scottish periphery – and this reluctance is a long-standing one, typified in the introduction to the Earl of Rosebery's *List of Persons Concerned in the Rebellion*.

Lord Rosebery initially states that Charles's force 'was essentially an army of clans' with 'no doubt, some few non-juring Episcopalians', before being forced to admit that in the words of its editor (Rev. Walter MacLeod), the names are 'insufficiently Celtic: hinting indeed that the Highland host is something of a phantom'. This is inconvenient: as Burke said, the nature of things is a sturdy adversary. But the Earl is unbowed. Having first stated that the list is deficient (which it is), he goes on to make the most revealing claim: that 'Scotsmen north of the Forth in 1745' were 'essentially Highlanders'. Apart from making one wonder why *The Wealth of Nations* was not written in Gaelic and why Archbishop Sharp did not habitually appear in the great plaid, this extraordinary remark indicates the domination of the marginalised Highland narrative of Jacobitism at that time. Yet Lord Rosebery still has facts in his defence when he states impressively that 'the eyewitnesses of the Pretender's army speak of Highlanders and nothing else'. On this basis, despite admitting that non-Highland levies joined after Falkirk, the Earl can confidently declare that 'the invasion of England was substantially a Celtic raid'.[15]

The fact that eyewitness accounts from the 1745 Rising itself appear to confirm that it was a clan affair might be explained by the confusion between Scots and Highlanders evident in eighteenth-century accounts and propaganda. But there is no need for such a speculative excuse. It appears that in 1745 Charles Edward and his field commanders took advantage of a powerful aspect of Jacobite propaganda: the idea of the Highlander as patriot, discussed in Chapter 1. The image of the poor but well-bred and militaristic Highlander as a symbol of historic Scottish patriotism, who placed his country before the lure of 'English gold', marched well with the classical images of (incorruptible) Roman Republicanism which were becoming associated with Charles Edward in the 1740s. The patriotic Highlander had become the equivalent of the English 'honest man' Jacobite code, and had indeed extended the use of tartan before 1745: the Englishman Sir John Hynde Cotton ordered a bespoke set in 1743 as a visible pledge of his Stuart patriotism. The Highlander was symbolic of commitment to dynasty, nationality and culture in ways which extended far beyond the Gaeltachd.[16]

It was against this background that the Jacobite forces were raised. This has not gone entirely unnoticed: a contemporary account of 'The Highlanders [sic] at Macclesfield in 1745' recalls 'a young Lowlander (but in a Highland dress)'; Frank McLynn tells us that Lowland units carried the targe, and Bruce Lenman, almost as an aside, states that 'Charles put all his men in Highland dress'. Lenman and McLynn may not be the only modern historians who make the point, but it is rarely made; both may be drawing on an important and neglected article on the 'Dress of the Jacobite Army', published by Sir Bruce Seton in the *Scottish Historical Review* of 1928. Sir Bruce draws on the same eyewitnesses as Lord Rosebery, but comes to a different conclusion:

> The important point . . . is that the witnesses drew no distinction between officers of Cromarty's, Lochiel's and the Grants on the one hand, and of Glenbucket's, Ogilvy's, or Roy Stewart's on the other. In other words the Highland–Lowland complex which appears to dominate the ideas of modern

writers on the '45 seems not to have existed in the minds of these eyewitnesses, on the accuracy of whose observation lives depended . . . We are driven, then, by the evidence of a court of law, to admit . . . that wearing the 'Highland habit' was, to say the least of it, a common practice among officers in the Lowland regiments.

Sir Bruce chooses to measure the statements of eyewitnesses against the regimental origins of those Jacobites testified against; in so doing, he confirms an army practice attested from other sources. Lord George Murray wrote on his departure from Carlisle that 'I was this day in my philabeg . . . without Britches . . . Nothing encourag'd the men more than seeing their officers dress'd like themselves.' In Scotland, Lord Lewis Gordon stated that he would be prepared to accept 'Highland clothes' in lieu of money from Aberdeen, while even more tellingly, Sir Bruce shows that the Manchester Regiment 'wore the white cockade, and a "plaid sash" or "plaid waistcoat"'. On 31 October 1745, the Atholl whig Commissary Bisset wrote that of the 5000 Jacobites under arms at that time, 'two thirds be real highlanders and one third lowlanders, altho' they are putting themselves in highland dress like the others' (the number and proportion of Lowland troops subsequently rose). There is even evidence that French officers who landed on the east coast during the 1745 Rising wore Highland dress, perhaps 'as a Protection against the highlanders who joined us' and to 'avoid danger in travelling in red clothes'. Whatever the reason, they shared the main dress of the Stuart forces, which appears to have been cemented by the drafting of Highland companies to serve in mainly Lowland regiments, as in the cases of the Atholl Brigade, the Duke of Perth's and the Edinburgh Regiment: a similar pattern to that of Mar's 1715 Rising. Leaving aside for the present the question of whether there was a major division of consciousness between Lowland Episcopalians and Highlanders anyway (recent work on the Atholl estates suggests little social distinction, and Episcopalians, like Catholics, seem to have been benevolent towards Gaelic), it is clear that Highland clothes formed a kind of uniform for a significant part of the Jacobite forces in 1745–6. In

establishing this, an element of genuine confusion which has succoured the Myth of the Jacobite Clans is removed. The ideological
elements of that myth are more elusive, and are best circumvented
by a detailed examination of the nature and extent of Jacobite military support in Scotland.[17]

The apparently small size of the Jacobite army can seem to confirm a narrow recruiting base and low level of support. There is of
course a *parti pris* for the status quo inherent in all assessments of
Jacobitism which measure its strength solely in terms of those prepared to risk all their property and a terrible death: on these terms,
we may ask if 400 IRA gunmen and a handful of INLA activists
represent the extent of nationalist support in Northern Ireland.
Leaving this aside, and acknowledging a significant number of part-
or full-time sympathisers (who may, or may not, according to taste,
be described as 'sentimental Jacobites'), it is still the case that the
Jacobite forces in 1745 were not as small as has been sometimes
assumed. Although Charles Edward led only 5000–6000 men into
England in the late autumn of 1745 (in addition to some 2000
women and camp-followers, twenty-one of whom were in prison
in Chester Castle by February 1746), there was a second army
being raised in the north. Even judging the strength of the Jacobite
forces by the maximum number in the field at Falkirk (8000–9000)
is not adequate, since no army engaged in holding territory to raise
men and money can put all its troops in the field. Lord Rosebery
estimated the total force at 11,000 (there are only 2520 names in the
List of Persons Concerned in the Rebellion), while more recently
McCann has suggested between 12,470 and 14,140 including
French and Franco-Irish troops (Hilary Kemp estimates there were
780 of these in the army 'on the eve of Culloden'). The habit of
historians of forgetting the northern army is perhaps exemplified in
the usually otherwise excellent work of Daniel Szechi, who does
not mention a figure for a Jacobite force exceeding 5000, and yet
still allows 4000 to rendezvous at Ruthven in Badenoch after
Culloden: clearly an army almost without casualties and desertion!
A careful estimate of the numbers involved also helps to undermine
another old *canard*, that 'undoubtedly more Scotsmen fought
against the Jacobites at Culloden than for them', oft-repeated and

not so often justified. Lord Elcho estimates 2400 Scots in Cumberland's army, including 600 Campbell militia; the Cumberland Papers give 2284. Both figures are under half the Jacobite force on the battlefield.[18]

Whatever the overall size of the Jacobite army in 1745 in the 11,000–14,000 range, it does show a decline from the army raised by Mar thirty years earlier. But both Mar's army of up to 20,000 and Charles Edward's force of between three-fifths and two-thirds as many compare not unfavourably with the numbers raised by the Scottish Covenanting administration in the 1640s – and this with the far greater difficulty and danger involved in raising men to fight for the Jacobites. Although the Covenanting armies were recruited a century before 1745, Scotland had suffered great hardships in the intervening 100 years. Economic decline and repeated famines, the most severe of which in the 1690s cut the population by between 5 and 33 per cent, depending on the estimate accepted, had done severe damage. In addition, perhaps up to 200,000 Scots emigrated to Ireland between 1688 and 1715. One population historian concludes that 'it is not impossible . . . that Lowland Scotland in 1691 had much the same population as it had in 1755'. Besides this, the era of the Covenanting wars had seen serious outbreaks of deadly epidemic:

> The outbreak of bubonic plague which hit the east-coast towns in 1645 was the most severe for two centuries. It accounted for two-thirds of the population of Brechin and more than half that of south Leith. Probably one in five town-dwellers died of it in 1645. Unlike other demographic crises, urban populations did not quickly recover: rents in Edinburgh were reduced by a third in 1651.

The figures for Brechin (from a petition to Parliament) may include mortality from other sources, but there is no doubt that the east-coast burghs suffered heavily, Aberdeen (including Futtie, Torry and Oldmachar) losing 1760 from 9000 in 1647. Despite such setbacks, the population had risen, but not by enough to invalidate comparisons (indeed, increases between 1691 and 1755 in the shires of Angus, Edinburgh and Kincardine are small, and other areas were virtually static: in addition, quite a significant portion of the Angus increase seems to take place between 1748 and 1755). Some of the actual increase in population was in the west Lowlands: the weakest Jacobite area of all, but strong for the Covenanters who had preceded them. In 1639–40, the National Covenanters, at the peak of their power, raised an Army of the Covenant totalling 23,000. In 1644, the Solemn Leaguers had 21,500, in addition to an army raised that June of between 6800 and 8000 under the Earl of Callendar. In 1648, the Engager Army was around 14,000–15,000 or more; in 1650, there were 23,000 in the forces at the time of Dunbar, when 2000–5000 had been purged from the army. The figure for 1651 did not exceed 21,000: 12,000 marched with Charles II to Worcester. This was an invasion force which, like his great-nephew's ninety-four years later, was joined by few Englishmen. Despite this, Charles II is not regarded as relying on the marginal representatives of a doomed culture: he later won, so teleology is satisfied.[19]

Such figures indicate that, even in the course of a prolonged and trying war effort, the maximum strength that the Scottish administration could expect to raise in the Covenanting period was around 25,000 men. There were, it is true, Scots serving abroad: but this was also the case in the eighteenth century. Moreover, a recent Covenanting scholar has judged 'that the Covenanters were good at raising armies, particularly when one realises that Scotland had not engaged in prolonged military activity since 1573 and had no established system of levying large numbers of troops' (Furgol, 1990, 4). Since the Scottish army when it existed after the Covenanting period was usually very small, that era appears even more unusual, and is perhaps indicative of maximum or near-maximum practical levels of mobilisation in early modern Scotland. If this is the case, 25,000 seems about the practical ceiling: a figure only briefly exceeded during the Covenanting wars, and which was higher than the number raised during the peak of national appeal in the Bishops' Wars. Nor were the royalist forces significant enough to qualify this figure markedly, as indeed I suggested was the case in Dundee's rising. Neither the 2000 raised in the north in 1639 nor the hardly much larger number of Scots in Montrose's forces weakened the national quality of the Covenanting armies opposed to them as much as Hanoverian sympathisers did that of the Jacobites in the following century. At no time in the Covenanting period could Scottish royalists recruit anything approaching the numbers raised by Mar and Charles Edward: many families who were later Jacobite were ardent in the Covenanting cause. In 1715 and 1745, Jacobite commanders levied forces of comparable strength to the armies of the Covenant themselves (exceeding them in some areas), and this in conditions of extreme difficulty and danger, where not only were money and arms scarce and the legitimacy of the cause in question, but also the frightful penalties of English treason law hung over all who rallied to the standard. If it would be too much to claim that the '15 and the '45 were truly national risings, they nonetheless possessed a national quality. Almost every county appears to have supplied some men for the army (even Ayrshire, though Rosebery doubted this), and there was Jacobite activity as far afield as Orkney.[20]

Turning to examine the geographical roots of Jacobite support in 1745, we find that far from the Rising being 'a predominantly Highland or even West Highland' affair, only some 43–6 per cent of total troop strength seems to have come from the Highlands (Jean McCann's estimate, borne out by Frank McLynn). On the other hand about 2000–3280 (17–24 per cent) came from Moray, Aberdeen and Banff, and 17–20 per cent from Perthshire (though this may possibly be an underestimate, as some Perthshire recruits may have served under different colours). Around 900 (7 per cent) came from Dundee and Angus and 450 (3.5 per cent) from Edinburgh and Hanoverian deserters by this estimate, leaving Irish picquets, south and west Lowland recruits, the Royal Scots and the Manchester Regiment to make up the final 7 per cent (c. 1000). This may understate the number of Franco-Scots and Franco-Irish troops involved, since it implies a figure of around 500, whereas *Prisoners of the '45* suggests a high of 1264 (600 Royal Scots, 489 Fitzjames's horse, 175 picquets), and Hilary Kemp, cited above, states that there were still 780 troops from the French service with the Jacobites in April 1746. Whatever adjustment in the exact figures may be necessary, this distribution clearly evidences a pattern of significant to heavy Jacobite support throughout northern Scotland. Both Highland and Lowland support had declined since 1715, but this appears to have been due to the actions of individual magnates as much as or more than to changing sympathies. For example, the loss of Huntly and the Lowland cavalry account for much of the reduced Lowland contingent, as the absence of Sir Alexander MacDonald of Sleat had an adverse effect on Highland numbers. The details of the recruitment pattern will be examined later.[21]

In 1745 as in 1715, the leadership of the Jacobite army was mainly in Lowland hands. Although Highlanders disproportionately predominated in the Council of War, which led to a central 'strategic importance' being afforded to their views (McCann, 1963, 107), they were in a minority not only on the Privy Council but by most other measures of political and military authority. Of 112 officers of field rank or above in 1745, only fifty-three were Highlanders, and this despite the established Highland military habit (mentioned with scorn by Sinclair in 1715) of attaching a colonelcy to small retinues. Similarly, of nine general officers, only one (Alexander Robertson of Struan) could be counted as a Highlander, and his rank of major-general was largely a courtesy. Other than Struan, the lieutenant-generals were the Duke of Perth and the Jacobite Duke of Atholl, Lord John Drummond and Lord George Murray; the major-generals were Viscount Strathallan and Gordon of Glenbucket, while Lord Nairne and Walter Stapleton were brigadiers. Only one of the five staff colonels and four of the nine aides-de-camp were Highlanders, as was a mere one of the seventeen Jacobite governors. The pattern continues among the ordinary commissioned officers: one tally suggests that of 290 such, forty-nine came from Edinburgh (fifty-five including Leith), thirty-eight from Aberdeen, thirty-six from Dundee, twenty-seven from Kirriemuir, seventeen from Perth, sixteen from Brechin, twelve from Inverness, eleven from Elgin, eleven from Arbroath/St Vigeans, ten from Montrose and eight from Stonehaven. This would mean that 80 per cent of officers were Lowland. At least forty-five Scottish towns with a population of over 1000 in Webster's 1755 census (about a third to two-fifths of the total, and up to half outside the west) provided officers for the Prince's army. Though lacking many of the major magnates of 1715, the Jacobite force nonetheless attracted the support of a significant number of the Lowland Scots nobility, including the Duke of Perth and Duke of Atholl (Marquis of Tullibardine in government eyes), the Earls of Kilmarnock, Kellie, Cromartie, Traquair, Newburgh and Clancarty (as well as, briefly, that of Nithsdale), Viscounts Strathallan, Frendraught and Dundee (briefly Kenmure) and Lords John Drummond, Lewis Drummond, George Murray, Forbes of Pitsligo, Nairne, Elcho, Balmerino, Lewis Gordon, Macleod, Ogilvy and Lovat (leaving aside those magnates with titles conferred by the exiled court).[22]

Significant evidence also exists for the number of men raised in each town and district in the Lowlands in 1745. Recruiting from towns in particular was difficult, and risky for the recruits: it was much harder to force men, and there were many witnesses, few of whom needed to be hostile to secure subsequent convictions. In such circumstances, it is remarkable that many urban areas supplied significant numbers of recruits, and that as a result of the circumstances of town life, many of these were volunteers. Out of a total of 220 from the Aberdeen area, only nine claimed to have been forced, as did a mere one from 112 in the Oldmeldrum and sixty-nine from 388 in the Elgin area. A mere six out of 406 from Fife and the southern Lowlands claimed forcing, as did one out of 138 Edinburgh recruits (McCann, 75–7, 99–100). Even a hostile historian admits that 'there was no pressing', or virtually none, in Dundee, though Annette Smith states that 'only 17 [of the Jacobites] are described as volunteers'. Such a formal description might well be more often applied to those who were gentleman-volunteers, and perhaps we would do better to regard the generality of those who were not forced as effectively voluntary recruits – in which case, in much of the Lowlands, particularly the Lowland towns, we are dealing with men in this category.[23]

Many of these soldiers were raised when Charles was in England, and seem to have continued to serve close to their localities. Before the Prince set out for the south, it was clear that the east-coast ports and hinterland were sympathetic: nearly 500 carts were found to transport artillery and supplies from the French ships which began to unload in the north-east at the beginning of October (the Stonehaven fishing fleet guided one of the transports in safely past a British man o' war). Intelligence reports (which, incidentally, suggest that the main Jacobite force was better armed than some have supposed) indicate that by the middle of November a core of 300 had assembled at Perth, while recruiting parties were out in Fife, Angus and Montrose. More were expected from the north: James Gordon the younger of Aberlour had already raised two companies in Banffshire, while Crichton of Auchengoul (Viscount Frendraught) was recruiting in Aberdeen: he eventually raised about a company there. Within four days there were 700 men reported at Perth, with 400 to come. In another three days, 800 had landed at Montrose under Lieutenant-General Lord John Drummond, and reports were coming to Aberdeen (where there were 260 troops by 26 November) of 150 French landing at Stonehaven. By early December, it was stated that the army on the east coast was 3000 strong, with 300 at Aberdeen, 500 at Arbroath, 100 at Montrose and 100 in the Mearns. Within a further week there were 300 at Stonehaven, 200 at Brechin and 700 at Dundee, out of a total force estimated by Scottish Hanoverian agents on 13 December at 3450, and by General Blakeney's intelligence at the same time at 3300. The Jacobites apparently claimed 6000, though these could not all have been effectives: on 27 November, the Rev. Bisset heard at Aberdeen that the northern army had reached 4920, and it certainly grew no larger than this, if indeed it was as big. Lowland Scotland north of the Tay was an area where considerable Jacobite support was forthcoming, much of it from small towns and their environs whence the risk of volunteering was high. Many of these men joined the main army after the Battle of Falkirk, though others continued to serve in the localities.[24]

It has been argued that Jacobitism was less popular in the towns in 1745 than in 1715, because the administration did not oversee the election of sympathetic magistrates, but instead resorted to military rule. As Bruce Lenman says, 'Whereas in 1715 the Jacobites were able to hold elections to confirm their grip on the east-coast burghs north of the Tay, in the '45 Charles had to simply appoint governors of the major burghs' (1980, 257). This may have been done to some extent in order to maximise recruitment, perhaps more efficiently realised in the later rising than in 1715. The reports of contemporaries concerning the sympathies of the burghs are mixed. Cumberland thought that few were well affected in Edinburgh and suspected widespread collaboration: Jacobite sympathies were thought to be 'still rampant' in 1746. Certainly, the records of the guard after Hanoverian forces reoccupied the capital show that there were persistent cases of pro-Jacobite unrest among the men until late February 1746, well after the Prince's army had retreated out of the reach of any would-be volunteers. In the environs of Edinburgh, 'many people in East Lothian . . . were Jacobites', while unrest in the capital itself continued for a number of years. On 20 December 1748, Charles Edward's birthday (and the year in which Hume published the *Enquiry Concerning Human Understanding*), 'the Lion, the crest of the Scots arms placed above the outer entry of the Parliament House . . . was found dressed in a white wig and a blue bonet [sic] . . . the mob (a very numerous one) cried several times "Huzza! huzza! the blue bonnet has won the day! the blue bonnet has won the day for ever!"' 'One of the eyes' of Cumberland's picture on the Crown Tavern signpost 'had been scraped out', and the crowd cried 'that Cumberland has gratten out baith his een to see the lion better busked than himsell'. A bonfire was lit on Salisbury Crags, and between forty and fifty marched down 'the Canongate to the Abbay gate' in 'blue bonnets, with white cockades'. This was behaviour in keeping with the 'riotous' entry of Charles Edward in 1745, when the '"common people" and the women' flocked to him. Indeed, the belief that women tended to be almost universally Jacobite seems to have been quite widespread. An Edinburgh Whig memorandum of the time, which claims to be 'An Impartial and Genuine List of the Ladys on the Whig . . . or . . . Jacobite Partie', enumerates 194 Whig and 134 Jacobite ladies in Edinburgh and environs in its attempt to lay this story to rest: in its pride that over half of the ladies of note were Whig, it reveals the strength of Jacobite feeling. If its contemporary opponents were prepared to concede Jacobitism 44 per cent support among some of the movers and shakers of Edinburgh opinion, what price the marginal movement of clansmen, sidelined by Lowland landowners and bourgeoisie? While there is no proof of there being majority support for the Jacobites in Edinburgh, it was clear that there was significant sympathy. This continued, as disaffected meetings were to be found in Leith until at least the early 1750s, while in the 1770s the Jacobite Episcopalian congregations were still counted in hundreds.[25]

It was estimated that 'full two-thirds of the two towns of Aberdeen were very well-affected to the Government': Old Aberdeen was reported to show 'a more than ordinary zeal'. While the town as a whole was accounted 'by the farr greatest part very Loyall' by some, on the other hand there was the wildly optimistic view of the Jacobite *Caledonian Mercury*, which claimed on 7 October 1745 that 'the whole free-holders of Aberdeen (four only excepted) have actually declared for the Prince's interest'. Whether or not it was the case that the city was 'overaw'd by the Rebells', there was little sign of Hanoverian activity during the Jacobite occupation. It was believed at the time of the Battle of Inverurie that Lord Loudon's militia supposed that 300 in Aberdeen would rise in their support: if so, they were sadly mistaken. Just as telling as the inactivity of Hanoverian supporters during the 1745 Rising may be that of the Jacobites after it. As late as 3 July 1746, it was reported that, both in Edinburgh and Aberdeen, 'they [the Jacobites] continue prodigious insolent'. On 1 August, as the windows and inhabitants of Aberdeen were stoned by the occupying troops, the Earl of Ancrum declared it 'this infamous town'. After all, had not the Aberdeenshire and Banffshire Jacobites done 'more harm than all the Highlanders put together' in the north-east of Scotland?[26]

In Dundee and Perth, matters stood less well for the Jacobites in 1745. Pro-Stuart sympathisers there were in a minority, not a small minority perhaps, but not enough to keep the towns quiet without armed force. Charles Edward attended Episcopal worship at St John's, Perth; but this was apparently not enough to swing the town behind him. It was reported to the authorities that 'there are many in Dundee who would willingly bring out things against Jacobites and against the present administration for skreening them', and this was clear from their behaviour. On 30 October 1745, Hanoverian mobs besieged Oliphant of Gask, depute governor of Perth, and chased the governor of Dundee, David Fotheringham, out of town. Subsequently, both towns were heavily garrisoned. By late November 1745 there were reported to be 'just now in Dundee about 1000 Highland [sic] men a great many of them raised in Angus by Sir James Kinloch', and there were, besides, 'a great many Highlandmen in Perth I can't tell exactly how many'. Yet despite the need for such watching parties, both towns made a significant military contribution to the Jacobite cause in 1745 which was not at all out of keeping with the numbers raised there for earlier armies: in comparison with the town's contribution in the Covenanting period, Dundee in 1745 was not particularly backward, although few of any substance were active Jacobites. Moreover, it is clear that, given the presence of strong Hanoverian sympathisers in the town, they were brave men who volunteered. Annette Smith suggests that 'we cannot know whether they were persuaded to join by the attractions of Ogilvie's men's smart red and black uniform', but this is surely (given the risks) unnecessary derogation, typical of the marginalisation of Jacobitism as a matter of serious political choice (Smith, 1988, 107–8).[27]

Although by the end of November 1745 some 1190 of the estimated 1263 Jacobite troops at Perth were indeed Highlanders, the garrisons at Dundee and elsewhere were very markedly Lowland (and not therefore an 'occupying Highland force' (Smith, 108)). If the smaller towns south of the Forth were difficult to recruit from despite the perceived sympathy of their inhabitants (Lord George Murray wrote to the Jacobite Duke of Atholl from Linlithgow on 15 September 1745 that 'the Low country people seem to be much in our interest, and, were it not for our marauding, I believe we would be welcome guests'), the same was not always true further north. While the inhabitants of Dunkeld were regarded by one exasperated Jacobite as 'quite degenerate from their ancestors' because a company of sixty could not be raised there (there was eventual resort to forcing, perhaps by using 100 Frasers), by 7 October it was reported that a company was being raised at Montrose. Shortly afterwards, Lord John Drummond landed his

Royal Scots at the port. In November, government intelligence reported 140 at Montrose, while on 22 January 1746 it was said 'that Wallace of Arbroth [sic] & Erskine of Montrose have within these Eight dayes raised about 300 men that [were] never in arms before all Lowlanders'. On his march into Scotland, it was made clear to Cumberland that Brechin contained but a 'Small Number of the well Affected', and that troops were required to safeguard government supporters in the town. In this 'intensely Jacobite shire', Arbroath folk customs long recalled the 'hungry Hessians' later billeted on them by the government. In one game played by girls, King George's men ask for 'bread and wine', which they are not given:

> What care we for King George's men,
>> King George's men, King George's men;
> What care we for King George's men,
>> Cam a teerie, arrie ma torry.[28]

Further north it was said that 'Banff and the Seaport towns betwixt it and Aberdeen were mostly all dissaffected [sic]', and this was also true further south in Stonehaven and Johnshaven, as well as some of the inland towns: Jacobites were reported 'thickest about Carnousie, Achmedden, Pitsligo, Fraserburgh, Altri in Old Deer Parish, Inverugy, Fyvie, Monwheiter'. Robert Cunningham's report to the Earl of Crawford reveals how little reliance the Hanoverians placed on protestations of loyalty which may have satisfied later historians. Writing in the aftermath of Culloden, Cunningham warns that

> what is still more extraordinary, every one thought themselves obliged to put on the Appearance of being pleased, altho' their neighbours well knew they were otherways affected. In the little Town of Keith [in] Strathbogie, all was gayly & good humour, expressed by Ringing of Bells, Bonefires, & drinking of Healths, so much were they Convinced of the Total Defeat of their Friends.

Shortly, it seems, spirits improved, for on 10 June 1746 it was reported 'that the Jacobite gentlewomen of Montrose . . . got on white gowns and white roses, [and] made a procession through the streets', while Jacobite bonfires were lit.[29]

Such signs of disaffection continued for some considerable time. In January 1747, it was stated that 'the Inhabitants of all that Country [Badenoch] are living peacably [sic] at home, save a very few who never Surrendered and all of them as fond of a Rebellion . . . they . . . still keep the fresh good Arms'. Similarly, it was said that 'the People of Aberdeenshire . . . are in Readyness to embrace a Rebellion'. On 15 February 1747, it was reported that 'the Expectations of the Disaffected encrease daily'. These were supported by the continuation of a guerrilla campaign by elements in the Jacobite forces long after Culloden. In the first few months after their defeat, significant groups remained in the field under Lochiel and other commanders, James Campbell informing the Earl of Crawford on 26 April that there was a force of 120 Jacobites reported near Balquhidder. Even considerably later, fragmented units survived. On 23 September 1746, the Presbytery of Brechin applied for protection against insurgents who were harrying round Edzell, while on 7 March 1747 'two Rebel officers of Lord Cromartie's Regiment' came to Dingwall with sixteen or seventeen armed men to abduct Murdoch Mackenzie, a former fellow-officer. Afterwards they were joined by more troops on 'the Hill above Dingwall'. Throughout areas sympathetic to Jacobitism, this was by no means unusual, as the many outposts maintained by the British Army confirm. In summer 1756, for example, there were still fifty-five patrols in and bordering the Highlands: these were divided into five detachments, of which each was a captain's or subaltern's command. Trouble as far from the Great Glen as Angus was clearly still expected, as the Kirriemuir patrol consisted of a subaltern, sergeant, corporal, drummer and twenty men: a larger group than was deployed in most places in the Highlands.[30]

Various figures are available for the numbers raised in Lowland towns and localities. Although these must be picked through with some care, they are usually fairly consistent in their indications. If this is not the case, it may be that a different measure is being used: parish rather than town, or the inclusion of environs. No two figures for Edinburgh's contribution agree, but there is nonetheless a fair degree of consistency. The Jacobite muster roll gives 118 names (including Broughton), Rosebery's incomplete list 126, and 138 is the figure from McCann's 1963 survey. Given the absence of any claimed comprehensiveness from the first two, McCann's is likely to be the closest figure. In any case, the numbers raised are roughly equivalent to the size of the force defending the town of Edinburgh against the insurgents, which stood at 124 on 9 September 1745, though by the 15th 700 had at least notionally been raised for that task (400 of these mustered, though when it came to the prospect of fighting, they dwindled to forty-two). Thus the Jacobite force recruited from Edinburgh was of a fair size; on the other hand it fell far short of the regiment which the city raised (the only burgh to manage this feat) for the Covenanters, which numbered almost 500 a century before. Jacobite hopes of providing an Edinburgh Regiment entirely from the town proved optimistic, despite its population of 50,000: it was the second-largest city in Britain, and much bigger than either Norwich or Bristol. Instead, the force that bore that name came one-third from the city, and was two-thirds composed of Hanoverian deserters and other makeweights, such as the twenty-three raised by the Earl of Kellie, a Jacobite colonel better remembered for his music. The forty-nine officers whom Edinburgh may have provided indicate proportionately high support among the better off: when only 1 per cent of the UK population was in the professional middle class or above, over a third of Edinburgh Jacobites were in this category, and this was not always untypical of other centres of Jacobite recruitment.[31]

It can be argued that this display of somewhat narrowly-based and moderate support was out of keeping with the strong welcome which the Prince received in the capital. The Jacobites reported little antipathy in the town, leaving aside the ubiquitous desire of the tradespeople to overcharge; and it may be that recruitment was adversely affected by the Castle's remaining in British hands, especially when the governor threatened to bombard the city in response to Jacobite blockade. On the other hand, despite strongholds such as Old St Paul's (where Thomas Ruddiman, David Hume's predecessor as Keeper of the Advocates' Library, was a member of the congregation) and Leith, Episcopalianism was weak in Edinburgh – and the presence of large numbers of Episcopalians was usually the best predictor of strong Jacobite recruitment, while despite the presence (according to a government estimate) of over 6000 Jacobite troops, accession to the army in the city was slow and at a weak level. By contrast, government agents estimated total Jacobite recruitment in the shires of Edinburgh and Stirling 'and other places over and above' at 1000 men. In summary, the capital, with one in twenty of the Scottish population, provided only one in 100 of the Jacobite army. Nevertheless, this was still a significant contribution; and the unrest after the Jacobite forces departed indicates that, if not a heartland of disaffection, the city was still a powerful source of it. On 23 April 1746, Cumberland told Newcastle that Jacobite colours were to be burnt by the common hangman in Edinburgh, 'as that town has been so very ill affected'.[32]

In Aberdeen's case, there are wide variations in the eight (at least) estimates of those actually raised. At the low end, the burgh records suggest a figure of sixty-nine; but the muster roll gives 110, and Rosebery 117, including Oldmachar. McCann's estimate of 220 from the city and environs is still lower than the 263 identified by the Taylers. A figure of around 200 for Aberdeen and environs is probably fair: there are many reasons for official records to minimise embarrassment and protect individuals, especially if levels of recruitment were high. On the other hand, the Taylers' figures include all those associated with Jacobite sympathies in the period of the 1745 Rising. The masters at Aberdeen Grammar School who stopped praying for King George certainly had such sympathies, but apparently never took up arms.[33]

Recruiting in and around Aberdeen was successful enough to provide a battalion under the command of Lieutentant-Colonel James Moir of Stoneywood, and this was apparently a volunteer unit: 'Stonywood however found enough about the town of Aberdeen and places adjacent without force', records a hostile witness. In addition, Viscount Frendraught (Crichton of Auchengoul) successfully raised men for Lord Lewis Gordon's regiment. Although the Rev. John Bisset recorded that he was 'ravished to hear that, when the [recruiting] drum beats, not a few of the boys cry God save King George!' and there was crying against James in the streets, many indubitably came out, and did so willingly. To some extent, the anxiety of north-eastern Jacobites over recruitment, evident in Erskine of Pittodrie's letter to Colonel Moir, that 'as for raising of men, I see such a backwardness, it will be the greatest force that will bring them out', can be explained as the product of a need to maximise mobilisation in the face of a Presbyterian opposition which appears to have strengthened markedly since 1715. Certainly, it hardly squares with the fact that only nine out of 220 in the Aberdeen area are reported as complaining of forcing. Though Stonywood initially recruited 'supported by a couple of broken merchants and York street Cadys' (Taylers, 1934, 357), and 200 of his men are supposed to have deserted en bloc near the end of the campaign, he was nevertheless in the main successful in capitalising on considerable Jacobite sentiment in Aberdeen and its environs: an example of this is the countrymen of Bucksburn's accession to the army on its march to confront Loudon at the Battle of Inverurie on 22 December 1745.[34]

At the time of the Rising, Aberdeen was a town of 11,000 or 12,000 people, probably significantly larger than it had been a century before. During the Covenanting period, it had been the only burgh which did not join the opposition to the Prayer Book in 1637, a stance long held to be inspired by the group of clergy known as the Aberdeen Doctors. After the wars over the Covenant began, it proved difficult to recruit men in the city. In 1640, Aberdeen 'put up stiff resistance to providing [the Earl] Marischal with 110 men (or possibly two companies)'; 'Old Aberdeen supplied twenty men under duress'. By October 1640, 1200 had deserted Marischal's Covenanting regiment, probably anti-Covenanters from Aberdeenshire and the Mearns (Lord Gordon fared even worse: in 1644, 2600 of his 3000 muster deserted the standard of the Covenant). Thus even the presence of the most powerful local magnates could not secure lasting local support, and fewer men from Aberdeen stayed with their colours than fought for the Jacobites in the following century. In 1644, the magistrates of the town had to press twenty-eight men to reach the burgh 'quota of 120 soldiers, ten officers and a captain'. Although 500 men in the Burgh Foot mustered on the links in 1644, this probably had more to do with the imminence of Montrose and its likely effect on the town than with any sudden conversion to the cause of the Covenant (similar doubt may be cast on the sincerity and effectiveness of the 'several companies of militia' raised in the wake of the Duke of Cumberland's visit, especially in the context of militia strength and performance elsewhere in Britain in 1745). In the course of 1649, Aberdeen provided only thirty men, and only another thirty in 1650, leaving the burgh 'still deficient by sixty men in early September' of that year in its contribution to Viscount Arbuthnot's foot (a unit which may never have been properly raised). Assessed for ninety men in 1650–1, Aberdeen only managed to produce them on 21 August in the latter year. The Covenanters thus found repeated difficulty in raising men, and their success did not match that of their Jacobite successors, despite the greater stability, greater perceived legitimacy and financial security which allowed their regime to recruit intensively over long periods of time. Even taking into account the fact that it might be harder to raise men at the end of a long war than at the beginning, Covenanting achievements in levying the north-east were modest. The 310 men required by the Committee of Estates from Aberdeen and Banff shires in 1650 does not compare particularly favourably with the 1183 recorded by the Taylers from the Rising of 1745. As the Rev. Bisset gloomily predicted, 'if the rebels at Carlisle return not to Scotland, the seat of the rebellion . . . is like to be in Perth, Angus, Merns, Aberdeen, and Banff shires'.[35]

Notwithstanding this opinion, the north-eastern gentry seem to have been a deal cooler ('not one fourth of what they were') than in 1715. If the gentry had declined, however, recruitment from the lower orders of society, who continued to dislike the malt tax and probably the remote government which levied it, remained strong, as will shortly be made clear. Marischal was of course absent in France, and there was no Huntly, Mar or Panmure to appear in the Jacobite interest. Nonetheless, with the exception of the loss of Huntly's troops (the cavalry in particular), recruitment held up very well. In addition to Aberdeen's contribution, around two companies (forty-five according to the Muster Roll, sixty-four according to the Taylers) came from Banff itself. Captain David Tulloch of Dunbennan required 200 of the town, but gained only sixty to eighty. Several companies came from the surrounding shire: two were raised by Lord Forbes of Pitsligo and two by James Gordon the younger of Aberlour. John Hamilton of Sandiestown raised almost 100 near Huntly, consisting of seventy foot and twenty-five horse, while Patrick Duguid of Auchinhove recruited a company of thirty to forty from Lumphanan in November 1745 (Jacobite companies, not unlike Covenanting ones, had a tendency to be under strength, and could number as few as ten, as the Appin Regiment's order book makes clear: the regiment had eight companies totalling 280 at one muster). Working at this level, a company's strength came from each of Oldmeldrum, Fochabers, Turriff and Ellon, and slightly fewer than this (including sympathisers) from Aboyne, Cruden, Keith and Fraserburgh. Banchory, Portsoy, Carnousie, Huntly, Durn, Inverurie, Rayne and Peterhead all provided significant handfuls (sympathy in Peterhead in particular was clearly very strong), while almost every settlement of any size in Aberdeenshire and Banffshire provided some recruits for the Jacobite forces. Although this did not match the spectacular recruitment gained by the movement from the Angus coast, it is nevertheless plain that there was very significant sympathy and support for the Jacobites in north-east Scotland. The numbers raised in Aberdeenshire and Banffshire were sufficient to form five battalions, as well as that body of cavalry known as Pitsligo's horse.[36]

During the Covenanting period, Dundee had usually been assessed at two companies (notionally 200 men, though – as stated above – Covenanting companies frequently dipped to Jacobite levels): this was the assessment on the town for the Army of the First Bishops' War in 1639. Dundee had its quota lowered to 150 on appeal during the Engagement, but the burgh did not meet this reduced figure: only ninety were raised in total, and it took three weeks to find even thirty men. Two companies were raised by the Army of the Covenant in 1648–50, but it took half a year to recruit 170. Thus, even though ten companies had been raised from southern Perthshire and the presbytery of Dundee in the Solemn League and Covenant campaign, the burgh itself exhibited repeated difficulty in matching recruitment targets.[37]

In 1745, two or three under-strength companies were raised in a few weeks. The exact number recruited from Dundee is unknown, but the available figures converge considerably more than in the case of Aberdeen, and indicate a total of around 80–100 (the Muster Roll, for example, gives eighty-nine names). Nevertheless, as indicated above, anti-Jacobite feeling in Dundee was strong enough to put the governor of the town to flight, and, surely partly as a result of this, several hundred of the northern army went to Dundee in November, where there were already 200 deserters from the Forfarshires assembled. Although a stronger minority than in Edinburgh seemed to favour the Stuarts with their military efforts, Dundee was no Jacobite stronghold.[38]

The case was otherwise with the towns of Angus and Mearns, particularly those on the coast. Angus, 'that loyal shire', as the Jacobite agent George Lockhart of Carnwath called it in the 1720s, was a heartland of Lowland Jacobitism. Arbroath, really quite a small town with a population of less than 2000 (3500 including St Vigeans) provided two companies for the Forfarshire Regiment. The Muster Roll and other sources give around forty-three to forty-seven names, but there is evidence that the number raised was considerably higher: accepting the companies as under-strength, around eighty seems a fair estimate of Arbroath's contribution. Captain John Erskine, brother to Lord Dun, raised two companies in Montrose, which are reported to have been of full strength (100 each), though we have no record of more than sixty individuals from the town and 179 from the district (Montrose had a population of around 4000 at the time). Since many of the Forfarshire Regiment disbanded in an orderly fashion after Culloden, it is possible that we do not have individual records of all its recruits, particularly those of the second battalion, largely raised by men such as Captain Erskine, Captain Wallace of Arbroath and Captain Ferrier of Brechin (who is again reported to have brought in two companies of 100 each) while the main army was in the south. Government agents (cited above) claim 300 raised by Wallace and

Erskine, presumably in addition to the 150–200 who had gone north to join the fight at Inverurie the preceding month. Brechin itself (a city of about 3000 at the time) probably raised near to 100 men, as we have records of almost seventy names.[39]

Both Forfar and Kirriemuir also lent major support to the 1745 Rising. The former provided at least one company (forty to fifty men), while Kirriemuir probably raised two (over fifty-five men: the Muster Roll gives thirty-five names, and other sources more). Further north, the Mearns coast was fertile ground, with Stonehaven and Dunnottar yielding two companies (forty-nine to fifty-five men). Johnshaven, regarded as totally Jacobite and despoiled by Cumberland as a result, provided a solid handful of recruits, while Laurencekirk received 118 carts laden with Jacobite supplies landed at Montrose, which, with Stonehaven, was a safe port. The rumoured sophistication of Jacobite artillery was a matter of some concern to government agents: they had 'six brass cannon of 4 pounders which they say will fire 11 times in a minute', as the intelligence from Dalkeith put it on 30 October 1745.[40]

One of the interesting features of the strong Jacobite showing from Angus and the Mearns was that the Covenanters had also done rather well over most of this area, Montrose raising over 4000 in 1639. Although the total force raised by the Jacobites did not match this figure, they appear to have had what may have been majority support throughout the Angus towns and on the Mearns coast: certainly these provided safe havens for their shipping, and as far as known, the transport convoys sent inland went unmolested.[41]

Perthshire, also a strong Jacobite area, raised far fewer urban recruits. It has been argued that those who rose in the county of their own volition usually did so because they had a personal tie to the Atholl house or lands, or because they were Episcopalians – and Perthshire had considerably fewer of these than Scotland north of the Tay. The Atholl correspondence seems largely to bear out this assertion: the networking of this great magnate family was clearly responsible for a great many recruits. In this context, the report that twenty-eight out of thirty-five lairds between Perth and Loch Lomond were Jacobites shows the solidarity of the gentry, unmatched in urban areas: almost the reverse of the situation in the north-east. Although a brigade of four battalions was raised, mainly off Atholl lands, Perth itself provided only a company's strength from a population of 9000. Towns such as Crieff and Auchterarder had many inhabitants who remembered 1715, when Mar had persuaded a reluctant James to allow them to be burnt in pursuit of a futile scorched-earth policy. Crieff nonetheless yielded a significant number of recruits; but not one town outside Perth seems to have managed to provide a company, Callander and Dunkeld coming closest to doing so. There were frequent difficulties in recruitment, for which significant recruiting parties were repeatedly required and less often forthcoming. The Jacobite Duke of Atholl's problems in gathering men together appear to have helped delay the Prince's march into England. Despite these difficulties and the reluctance of the towns to participate, Perthshire raised nearly 3000 men, almost a quarter of the Jacobite army – a level of recruitment which must count as very strong support, though a good number of these men were Highlanders (it is hard to be sure exactly how many). Quite possibly the increasing solidarity of nationalist-leaning Presbyterians behind Hanover had an effect on Jacobite recruiting in the Lowland areas of the county, given its lower level of Episcopal strength.[42]

In 1715, the Master of Sinclair raised a cavalry force of about ninety from Fife, and there was considerable enthusiasm for James there, particularly in the small East Neuk ports. In 1745, levels of support remained reasonable, though far below the ten companies raised for the Earl of Crawford-Lindsay in the Covenanting cause in 1643, or the ten foot companies raised from the parishes round Kirkcaldy and Dunfermline by the Earl of Dunfermline in the same cause (to say nothing of Balcarres's four troops of horse). In and round St Andrews yielded forty-four men, or a company: the city proper seems to have volunteered less than a quarter of this. Kirkcaldy and Dunfermline each provided rather less (perhaps a company between them: Lord Elcho's foot, raised in Kirkcaldy, had recruited 350–700 in June/July 1640). Twenty-seven names are given from Anstruther, while the only other town which provided even half a company was Cupar. Elsewhere, contingents were measured in handfuls: Crail provided ten men, and although a number of other towns gave individuals or tiny numbers, in overall terms recruitment was narrowly based, as an examination of the Muster Roll bears out. In all, Fife yielded only about 120 men (or three companies) in 1745. Since Dunfermline (for example) had a population of about 8000, this indicates no particularly strong or fanatical support; on the other hand, there was a definite Jacobite presence in Fife, and those who joined the Prince's forces were volunteers, as was also the case in the Lothians and Stirlingshire:

> From Edinburgh, Haddington, Dunfermline and Stirling, a large proportion of those joining were either tradesmen, craftsmen or workmen. These men came from classes upon whom no economic pressure, of the kind found in the Highlands, could be exerted, and joined presumably for personal or private financial reasons. Their adherence was apparently voluntary – few complained of being forced out and none of being hired out.[43]

In other words, even if the level of recruitment in these areas was relatively low (around forty-six came from the Stirling area and fifty-nine from the Haddington area according to McCann), it was still significant in the sense that recruits were willing to risk the loss of lives and fortunes for the Stuart cause. Not only was 'coming out' from towns risky, as indicated above: it grew riskier as the overall strength of Jacobite support declined. In the event of defeat, not only was the Jacobite soldier from these places more vulnerable to delation, but he also lacked the places to hide or the sympathisers to turn to whom he might have had in Banff or Angus. Thus apparently low levels of Jacobite support might nonetheless be significant.[44]

Recruitment from the Borders was very patchy: it is doubtful whether more than a company's strength acceded to the Jacobite forces from the whole area, no single location appearing to provide more than five men. This was far off the numbers raised in the Covenanting period. The western Lowlands and Campbell lands were, predictably due to their Covenanting inheritance, the weakest zones of support for the Jacobites. Two from Campbeltown joined the Prince's army, but the sole Episcopalian clergyman in Ayr was the only recruit from that burgh. Glasgow, with a population of 25,000 clearly the second-largest town in Scotland, did provide recruits, but only about ten or fifteen of them. Elsewhere, numbers were mostly counted in handfuls, though again it is worth pointing out that recruitment of a sort was achieved over a wide area of western Scotland. Lanark, Greenock, Hamilton and Dumfries all provided troops, half a company being raised in the last-named area. In total, Renfrewshire, Lanarkshire and Dumfriesshire produced about forty-seven Jacobite recruits, and here the contrast with the Covenanting period is, as might be expected, devastating. Lord Fleming's foot had raised 500 from Lanark; Viscount Montgomery's 300 from Renfrewshire; Ayrshire, Renfrewshire and Lanarkshire together provided 450 for the Earl of Eglinton's horse, while 1200 were raised for the Galloway foot 'from the Stewartry of Kirkcudbright and Wigtownshire'. The Earl of Cassilis's foot raised 1000 'from southern Ayrshire and Wigtownshire'. Whatever aid had been hoped for by the Jacobites from Cameronian quarters earlier in the century was clearly not now available.[45]

There were fragments of support elsewhere in Lowland Scotland. The reports of the Commissioners of Excise show that there were few places untouched by the Rising (one of these was Stranraer). As far afield as Orkney, there was Jacobite activity and several in arms. In Stromness, 'only James Grahame . . . late Baillie in Stromness . . . joined with the Rebells . . . in Robbing and plundering several Houses there. He went to Caithness with them, and returned again to this County where he sculks and lurks.' A very wise decision on his part, one might think! According to a report of 23 June 1746, six were in prison in Orkney, three had been released upon bail and a further five examined, presumably in addition to those who continued to 'lurk'. Although some of these may have been (as perhaps in James Grahame's case) taking criminal advantage of the general unrest caused by the 1745 Rising, there is nonetheless a variety of evidence of Jacobite activity far beyond the reaches of the Jacobite army or the main campaign.[46]

Three main constituent elements emerge in the pattern of Jacobite recruitment in the Lowlands. First, Jacobite support in 1745 rested on a broad geographical base, even where it was thinly spread. Second, in some areas it matched or even exceeded previous levels of recruitment which had sought maximum mobilisation in Scotland (while falling short in many others; nevertheless the total force bears comparison with Covenanting strength). Third, Jacobite heartlands almost exactly matched traditionally strong Episcopalian areas, and this was true to a greater extent in 1745 than 1715. Almost the whole of the coast and most inland areas in the strip of lowland running from Cromarty to Arbroath provided substantial Jacobite support, as did Perthshire outside the main towns (though here of course there was to an extent a mixture of Lowland and Highland recruits). The Lowland coast from Dundee to Edinburgh provided useful but not heavy support, Central Scotland and the Lothians a little, and the western Lowlands and Borders hardly 100 men. These areas had been more fruitful in Mar's Rising; but even thirty years later, it was clear that over much of Scotland there was a readiness to 'come out' which far exceeded the levels enjoyed by Viscount Dundee or the Marquis of Montrose. Jacobite support was at least in a shallow sense national, while regional strongholds readily matched or exceeded previous levels of mobilisation. Moreover, armed recruits were as always the tip of the iceberg, and towns which provided relatively few Jacobite soldiers were not necessarily by that token hostile (Peterhead provides a case in point, with strong sympathies but relatively few recruits). In few places outside the western Lowlands did the Jacobites receive the hostile reaction they found in Penrith. While expressions of sympathy with Jacobitism have a history of being treated with caution (no doubt often rightly so), its levels of mobilisation are impressive, if one leaves aside Webster's extremely optimistic rote estimate of 253,000 fencible men in Scotland, in his 1755 census, almost ten times the largest number that had hitherto ever been raised, despite the lists of up to 50,000 men supposed to be under the control of Scotland's magnates.[47]

Nor was the situation so different in the 1750s. In the Seven Years' War militia controversy, the size of a putative Scots militia was estimated at 6000–12,000, while lists of quotas of fencible men under the terms of the 'Assessment for the Execution of the Press Act' in 1756–7 give 165 as the figure for Aberdeenshire, 160 for Perthshire, 140 for Edinburgh, 102 for Forfarshire, 79 for Inverness-shire, 54 for Banffshire and 46 for Elgin. With due respect to the differing circumstances and aims surrounding these figures (which, of course, fall well short of maximum mobilisation), they once again tend to suggest that the Jacobite forces were good at raising men. If one compares the Jacobite army with the average size of British total mobilisation in the 1739–48 War of the Austrian Succession (62,373), it is clear that with less than one-fifth of the population, the Scottish force of 12,000–14,000 was by no means out of proportion. Admittedly, Britain had on occasion had more than 100,000 in the field in the early eighteenth century; but on the other hand, until the end of the seventeenth, the army seldom reached 30,000, and Mar provided two-thirds of this figure in Scotland in 1715. The 960 men recruited by the Duke of Gordon to fight in India in 1761 do not compare particularly well with the thousands raised by Huntly in the '15. At the outbreak of the American War of Independence, there were 48,000 men in the English and Irish establishments. Such figures put the Jacobite army in its proper perspective, as a significant military threat: its size should not be assessed on the basis of the mass mobilisations of a different age.[48]

Given that relative success, it is noteworthy that any examination of the correspondence of Jacobite commanders bears witness to their frustration in not being able to raise more: often due to reluctance, it is true, but also due to a lack of men free to recruit. There is also the lack of arms to consider. Though it appears that many of the Jacobites were well armed, it has been argued that more men could have been recruited if it had been possible to arm them: for example, Lochiel had to send Camerons home before Prestonpans due to an absence of weapons. Other reports support the view that this difficulty had a limiting effect on recruitment, as no doubt did the lack of money at times. On several counts, evidence exists which suggests that the Jacobite forces in 1745 could have been considerably stronger than they were, and that the army might even have approached its 1715 predecessor in size.[49]

It might be argued that the total strength of the Jacobite army, even given its high levels of Lowland support, benefited greatly from the Highlands, where figures of the availability of over 20,000 fighting men (though Patten lists only 10,220 for 1715/16) had been cited by government agents since the end of the seventeenth century. Sometimes such figures are quoted (no doubt by those who might be sceptical towards other assertions of Jacobite support) in order to demonstrate that only a small proportion of the Highlands actually supported the Prince. While it is true that many of the major magnates stood aloof, and that the most powerful clan (the Campbells) was overwhelmingly Whig, we should nonetheless question claims made concerning Highland military strength in the clan era. Highland armies were traditionally quite small, and nothing like the 20,000–30,000 sometimes claimed had ever appeared in arms; agents whose figures would at other times be questioned are believed on this point for the convenience of the historiography. Available forces in Scotland should be measured in terms of numbers who come out to fight, not numbers advertised or promised – as anyone writing about Jacobitism should be aware. Had the Mackenzies, the Macleods, Farquharson of Invercauld and MacDonald of Sleat come out for Charles in 1745, it is unlikely that he would have gained more than 3000 men, and that is a high estimate. In 1715, Seaforth had 1150 at Perth on 5 November, while MacDonald of Sleat had 650. Despite calculations that the latter could have raised up to 1000 for Charles (instead he brought out 200 for Hanover), MacDonald had not put two-thirds of that number in the field thirty years earlier.[50]

In 1715, the Camerons had brought out 600–700 men; in 1745, the figure was close to 1000, though as mentioned above, some of these had to be sent home. Clanranald had fielded 500–600 at Perth in November 1715, and Glengarry around 500, though eventually their joint force may have reached up to 2800 (McCann, 1963, 5): in 1745, Clanranald had 400 out (the Western Isles men did not come), Glengarry up to 1000. Macpherson brought out up to 1000 in 1715, and 350–400 thirty years later. The Appin Stewarts had 300 out in both risings, and the Frasers 600 in 1745, probably more than initially came out for Mar, while the Glencoe MacDonalds had about 100 in both risings. The Chisholms brought out about eighty in 1745, the Grants in the region of 100. Robertson of Struan had around 200–300 in both risings. Apart from Mackenzie, Macleod, Invercauld and MacDonald of Sleat, three battalions of Breadalbane men had also served in 1715, but were absent thirty years later. Leaving aside the missing magnates, only the Macphersons, Clanranald and Glengarry men showed marked decline from their numbers in 1715.[51]

There is another dimension to consider in any re-evaluation of the nature and extent of Jacobite support. There exists a traditional view, which we inherit, that the commercial classes would have nothing to do with the 1745 Rising: that the 'new' post-Union Scotland of middle-class tradesmen and professionals that was growing up in the Lowlands rejected Jacobitism totally. As R. H. Campbell puts it, 'the majority of Scots, especially those promoting and profiting from the reorientation of economic contacts', viewed the risings as 'unfortunate interruptions'. But it is by no means clear that this was the case. Out of a total of 695 recruits from north-east Scotland identified by McCann, 120 belonged to the gentry, and twenty-nine were professionals (fewer than in 1715, but still a good number when these formed a tiny proportion of the UK population), with 109 tenant farmers, fort-two merchants, 187 tradesmen and 208 labourers and servants. Analysis of the Taylers' list from the same area confirms the pattern almost exactly. Out of 757 names listed from Aberdeenshire and Banffshire who were involved in the 1745 Rising, there are 101 gentry, 179 professionals, merchants and farmers, 159 tradesmen and 318 from working-class occupations. In Angus, out of 825 recruits cited by McCann, 199 were tradesmen, forty-five farmers and 284 working-class; only fifty-seven of the total claimed to have been forced, perhaps rather surprising in view of the fact that this has been thought to be a major factor in the raising of the Forfarshires. Again, of 138 Edinburgh recruits, ten were gentry, thirteen professionals, seven other middle-class and sixty-seven tradesmen (given the number of officers who seem to have come from Edinburgh, some of the tradesmen were no doubt rather prosperous). The fullest occupational details that we have from the Muster Roll indicate that, in the two battalions of the Forfarshire Regiment, there were twenty-three merchants and 200 tradesmen among those whose occupation is recorded.[52]

Lists drawn up by the servants of government in the aftermath of the Rising also indicate a wide social spread in the army of 1745. The list submitted to the authorities of 'Persons in and about the District of Montrose Said to be Concerned in the Wicked and Unnatural Rebellion' gives 179 names: of these only four are gentry, a further forty-four prosperous middle-class, fifty-four less prosperous and seventy-five working-class. The 'List of those concerned that have Carried Arms and Aided and Assisted in the present wicked and unnatural Rebellion in or round Stonehaven in the Parish of Dunnoter [sic] and Fetteresso' gives only two gentry, eleven professional or prosperous middle-class, thirty-one more marginal and eleven working-class; again, it is the extent of middle-class involvement in the Rising which is interesting. A list of forty-six from Banffshire gives six gentry, twelve more and seventeen less prosperous of the middling sort, and eleven working-class; the thirty-six cited from Fraserburgh and environs likewise includes six gentry, eight more and ten less prosperous middle-class, and twelve working-class. From Dundee, a list of eighty names splits 11/14/22/33 along the same lines, while in the west the twenty-eight cited from Glasgow and Lanarkshire include five gentry, only one professional, twelve less prosperous middle-class and ten working-class. A list of seventy-three names from Aberdeen divides 10/21/21/20 (one unknown); in Anstruther, the twenty-seven names divide 8/8/8/2 (one unknown). These figures tie in with Frank McLynn's estimate of 316 gentry, 400 middle- and upper-middle-class and 1400 lower-middle- and working-class in the Jacobite army, though the final total will be higher than this (McLynn, 1983, 28).[53]

Such lists, especially where they are incomplete, will tend to show bias towards a higher proportion of gentry and well-to-do than was in fact the case, due to the higher profile which such members of society have. Yet even given this reservation, the numbers cited appear to bear out the contemporary contention that the lower orders of society did not proportionately favour the 1745 Rising with armed support (though this was not so much the case in Lancashire). Repeatedly, the numbers of the poorer sort listed are less than half, quite often less than a quarter of the total. What the figures do indicate is that the supposition that the Scottish middle class did not support the Rising appears not to be well founded: more than half of the Jacobites listed belonged to this group. Instead, it seems that the place of origin (whether one comes from a strongly Jacobite/Episcopalian Lowland area or not) is a better indicator of likely involvement in the Rising than social position. This may seem uncontroversial, since the Episcopalian nature of Jacobitism is very much part of the domain of discussion among sensitive historians; but accepting it undermines the notion of a primarily economic motivation common to all Protestants, as espoused by Linda Colley. It seems rather that we must accept that the confessional issue, localities and social expectation played a far greater part in determining the actions of Scots in 1745 than did their economic participation in the British state: after all, many prominent Jacobites were improvers or had significant mercantile interests, such as Cameron of Lochiel and Lord George Murray, and men like Bernard Ward or Colin Campbell lower down the scale. If family or marital links (as explored by Paul Monod) formed additional reasons for Jacobite activity, it nevertheless seems to have been the confessional issue which was paramount.[54]

The view of Jacobitism as marginal and belonging to an outmoded state of society which was practised by traditional historiography therefore wavers under scrutiny, as does its contention that the Rising found little support among the commercial classes. To take a sample of only a few individuals who were typical of Lowland Jacobitism's ability to recruit across a spectrum of society, there was Captain Charles Moir of the Aberdeen battalion, shipmaster in the town, and Captain Sandilands, a lawyer; one of the ensigns was a vintner, another a shoemaker and a third (Hercules Paterson) a surgeon and excise officer in Keith. Captain Robert Mitchell in Bannerman of Elsick's Mearns battalion was a brewer in Johnshaven; Walter Ogilvy, ensign in the Duke of Perth's, was a lawyer in Banff; George Bruce, sergeant-major in the Forfarshires, was a butcher in Brechin; sergeants William Wills and John Webster in the same regiment were a wright in Meigle and a mason in Kirriemuir respectively. Dougald Souter, private in Keppoch's, and an instance of the presence of Lowland troops in Highland regiments, was a messenger-at-arms from Edinburgh. While it is true that many tradesmen and others of the middling sort might be forced through circumstances of poverty or other private reasons to join the Jacobites, the pattern is too pronounced to allow of this being the main reason for these groups' part in the Rising of 1745. People who had a great deal to lose came out for the Prince, and these were not just the headstrong gentry of the old school, but from every rank, and especially the middle class in the Jacobite Lowlands of Scotland.[55]

Undoubtedly, the criminalisation of Jacobite activity and its subsequent alliance with other forms of criminal activity had an important role to play in socialising communities to Jacobite aims. Since the smuggling of key information, supplies and on occasion personnel was a central part of Jacobite activity, it was inevitable that the cause would become mixed with more conventional forms of smuggling. In addition to the natural intermingling of the different kinds of contraband traffic, conventional smugglers also provided a ready-made route of contact with the Jacobite community abroad and its purposes; they also benefited from Jacobite ambivalence towards Whig property law, given the doubtful legitimacy on which the ultimate property (the monarchy) rested. Jacobite connections with smugglers and highwaymen (some of whom praised the cause from the gallows or on occasion acted as its spies) were part of a cross-class interchange among those politically and economically (often two sides of the same coin) criminalised by the Hanoverian state. In Scotland, opposition to post-Union taxation changes ('Gentle and simple alike tended to resent the Customs and Excise service introduced into Scotland after 1707' – Lenman, 1984, 75) also helped to undermine confidence in the legitimacy of property relations, and the evasion of duties clearly provided a boost to smuggling. The east-coast ports were important in this, and their Jacobitism was probably fed by it. Episcopalianism was strong here, but it was so elsewhere where Jacobite support did not reach such very high levels: we should also surely attend to the link between disaffection and criminality in the Angus towns (Lenman, 1980, 216–17).

Even after 1745, these ports provided important routes of access to Scotland for the Jacobites, by this time exiles recruiting for the

French service, either the Irish Brigades or Lord John Drummond's Royal Scots, for whom 'recruiting . . . had gone on for several years . . . notwithstanding the utmost vigilance of the Government' (Allardyce, 1895/6, vol. 2, xx). The centrality of the east-coast ports in this scheme of things is borne witness to in a 1750 report on recruitment for the Brigades, which states that

> The generality of shipmasters in the Ports of Aberdeen, Peterhead, Aberbrothick [Arbroath], Montrose, Stonhive & Leith are disaffected, and have been from time to time employed in bringing disaffected persons to the Countrey & carrying them off again with recruits for the French service.

Recruitment of this kind (which the 1750 intelligence describes as 'a great encouragement to the revivall and progress of Jacobitism') continued until the French Revolution, being particularly prevalent along the Aberdeen and Banff coast. As in the 1750 expedition, exiled Jacobites could lead the recruitment parties. Jacobite and Jacobite-derived expatriates continued in the French forces for many years, one of the most famous being Marshal MacDonald, Duke of Taranto, of whom Napoleon said that 'he had no wish to test MacDonald's legendary loyalty by putting him within the sound of bagpipes'. MacDonald himself, on visiting Culloden, commented: 'those idiots of generals'.[57]

If the exiled community maintained a future of real military possibility abroad after 1745, the same was not true at home. Despite the odd piece of lingering guerrilla activity and the fiasco of the Elibank plot, Jacobitism posed much less of a threat than the building of structures such as Fort George would imply. The loss of that threat was due not just to the 'pacification' of the Highlands, but also to the crucial weakening of Lowland Jacobitism, hastened by the suppression of the Episcopal Church. The severe attacks on this confession in the aftermath of the Rising through penal legislation and direct violence ensured both an expansion in the number of licensed congregations with priests in English or Irish orders who did not acknowledge their nonjuring bishop, and the marginalising of that nonjuring element to an even greater degree. There were by 1755 perhaps only one-fifth as many Scottish Episcopal clergy with pastoral responsibility as there had been ten years earlier. This serious damage to the church was sparingly repaired in the nineteenth century; in the meantime, it deprived Lowland Jacobitism of a focus. By its own lights, the government had chosen the right target. This was not just because of Episcopalian support for divine-right ideology, for the church was a focus of a much more complex oppositionalism at the heart of any discussion of the national and nationalist qualities of Jacobitism, which will be reviewed in the next chapter.[58]

CHAPTER 3

Nationalists or Jacobites?

As the aversion to the Union dayly encreases, that is the handle by which Scotsmen will be raised to make a general and zealous appearance . . . as I am fully persuaded the better part of the English are far from thinking the Union beneficial to either Countrey, I cannot but see that it is expedient for the King to gratify his friends in Scotland.

Lockhart to King James, 18 December 1725

[T]he '45 was undoubtedly the last great National move in Scotland . . . the real movement . . . demanded a free Scotland . . . We must not be deceived by the ridiculous trappings with which our enemies have covered the great tale of the '45. It is a living issue and not a mere dead-end. The coming men will study it and its great men as the real Scotland.

F. W. Robertson

[T]he English and the Scots now agreed with each other ideologically, so that the English could allow the Scots themselves to police any threats to English peace. For example, the Scottish manager could be trusted with pacification of the country after the Jacobite rising of 1745–6 . . . securing not just

Scotland but Britain as a whole from what was felt to be the threat of continental despotism.

Lindsay Paterson

The plight of Scotland as I left her calls for your Majesty's close attention. That Kingdom is about to be destroyed and the English government is resolved to treat alike those who supported it and those who took up arms for me.

Prince Charles Edward Stuart, memorandum to Louis XV,
10 November 1746 [1]

D r Lindsay Paterson and Prince Charles Edward Stuart are not the only two writers on Jacobitism to disagree concerning its national dimension in Scotland. David Hume, who lined up with the vanishing Edinburgh militia in order to defend the capital on 15 September 1745, would hardly have been of a mind with F. W. Robertson as to the meaning of the Stuart cause for his country. Scottish history, particularly that of the sort which deals obliquely with the Jacobite phenomenon in pursuit of evaluating economic, social and intellectual development in central Scotland, tends to agree (in a general sense) with David Hume on this issue. Jacobitism as an atavistic and probably despotic sideshow to Enlightenment is a construct which belongs squarely in the Whig historical category dealt with earlier – and social and economic history is undoubtedly a strong redoubt of this school. By contrast, a modern 'four nations' historian such as Daniel Szechi understands very well that Jacobitism was an engine for Scottish nationalism well into the eighteenth century, even if the tone of such an assessment is more sceptical and downbeat than can be justified by the evidence:

Between 1689 and 1747 a dwindling number of Scotsmen struggled to maintain a separate, independent state. Hopelessly riven by religious antagonism, deep-seated political factionalism and particularist institutional interest groups, this proto-nationalist tendency was divided and bought off to maintain England's imperial dominance. Eventually only an uncompromising Jacobite-cum-nationalist minority remained. Denied any legal avenue of protest after 1714, this group in turn resorted to arms and was crushed militarily. (Szechi and Hayton, 1987, 259)

Such conclusions are not particularly controversial among revisionist historians and those writers on Scottish history who over many years have worked on re-examining the earlier consensus.[2]

Even so, the full implications of Jacobite nationalism have not always received the scrutiny they deserve. Although the romantic readings of the Myth of the Jacobite Clans also accepted the notion of a nationalist Jacobitism, it was one couched very much in terms of the recidivism of romantic clanship scorned by those sceptical mythologists whose sentiments were otherwise – as indeed I argued in the Introduction. Where such nationalism is acknowledged by more modern writers, it is seldom defined. For example, was this attitude to Scotland the property of all Stuart supporters, or only a section of them? How far was nationalism the major motivating factor in Scottish Jacobitism? Was it shared by the Stuarts themselves, and if so, what was their motive? Was it a matter of expediency or sincerity? And what kind of Scotland did the Jacobites want to see? Perhaps one of the reasons that these questions are seldom tackled is that they are more complex than they appear; what follows will thus be more in the nature of a preliminary investigation, and its conclusions will be tentative.

Although James VI and I had been an enthusiastic advocate of Union, it is perhaps less than accurate to align the 'Scoto-Britanes' of his reign with the unionists of a future age. His courtiers optimistically believed that Scottish values and mores could spread throughout the whole island when their king 'his brand all Britayne to obey sall bring', in the words of James's laureate, Alexander Montgomerie. James's attitude to Scotland was a complex one which can be treated either over-sympathetically or dismissively: on the one hand, his first twenty years of life gave him ample reason to dislike aspects of his country; on the other, he set out to deliberately develop a distinctively Scottish poetic court culture with its defining text on critical theory in the shape of James's *Reulis and*

Cautelis. As for the much-vaunted Anglicisation of Scottish writing in his reign, this has been shown to be at least as much the responsibility of the nature of the Scottish Reformation as of anything in James's court policy.[3]

Under Charles I and Cromwell, sections of English opinion, which had by and large been hostile to James's proposed measures, sought the effective reduction and Anglicisation of Scotland without the benefits of any properly negotiated union, such as the later Covenanters showed interest in. The Cromwellian 'union' was rather an ad hoc affair, never properly passed by the English Parliament; on Charles II's restoration, it slid into oblivion with the restoration of the Estates, Scottish Privy Council and judiciary. The return of the Scottish Parliament also led to a lowering of the crippling costs imposed on the country under Cromwell. By 1662, when the Restoration Settlement was effectively complete in Scotland, 'it was deliberate royal policy to keep the settlement of the three kingdoms apart from each other' (Lynch, 1991, 288).

Both Charles and James (the latter particularly during his sojourn in Edinburgh at the beginning of the 1680s) endeavoured to keep some sense of Scottish monarchy, carrying out significant works at Holyrood, endorsing the Scottish foundation-myth through the commissioning of the portraits of the royal line from Fergus for the same palace in 1684, and attempting to create a Royalist and Episcopalian culture in the Scottish capital. In pursuit of this, James both founded some of the institutions which may have underlain the subsequent development of the Scottish Enlightenment in Edinburgh, and also endorsed the antiquity and legitimacy of the Stuart line through antiquarian revivals, some of which had 'a distinctly pre-Reformation tinge'. Plans to expand the Scottish capital (which later resulted in the New Town) were first 'mooted' in the 1680s, 'with the encouragement of James VII' (Lynch, 353). From the beginning of James's exile, strong Jacobite support in Scotland and the potential of a successful rising there helped keep Stuart attention focused on their 'ancient kingdom'. Long before Union, James recommended in his advice to his son that Scotland as a free and ancient kingdom should be kept separate in its business from England. The king seems to have believed in 'a series of at least nominally equal kingdoms held together by royal authority' (Lenman, 1981, 57).[4]

After Union was passed, there was little sign of wavering on the part of the Stuarts in exile from this position, and encouragement such as Lockhart's was hardly needed. Apart from expediency and the possibility of principle, there was a strong reason for Stuart antipathy to the measure in that it was closely tied to the 1701 Act of Settlement, which had excluded them from the English throne. This was a confirmation of the 1688–9 settlement, which it has been argued that 'most Scots' saw 'as a piece of sharp practice whereby the English secured a Scottish settlement on the cheap without concessions'. The Act of Security that followed from the Scottish Parliament in 1703 sought to keep the succession in the two kingdoms separate, with the monarchy 'being always of the Royal LINE of Scotland . . . Providing always, That the same be not Successor to the Crown of England'. Despite the proviso that the Scottish monarch chosen would not be a Catholic, the Act of Security caused alarm in English government circles, and was as a result a direct *casus belli* leading to the Union, one effect of which was to extend the Act of Settlement to Scotland. Thus the Stuarts in exile regarded Anglo-Scottish Union as one of the constitutional mechanisms which had helped to dispossess them. Small wonder, then, that 'as to the Union the Old Pretender was represented as implacable' (G. H. Jones, 1954, 235). On 23 December 1743, James inveighed against the 'pretended Union', declaring that in Scotland 'We see a Nation always famous for valour, and highly esteemed . . . reduced to the Condition of a Province, under the specious Pretence of an Union with a more powerful Neighbour'. Charles Edward acted in similar vein in his time in Scotland (and did not disclaim such views after it, to judge from his November memorandum to Louis XV, quoted above). On 9 October 1745 in Edinburgh, he declared 'the pretended Union of the Kingdoms . . . at an End' (Lord George Murray was apparently unhappy at the high-handed nature of this proceeding, done as it was by decree). On 10 October, Charles released the following declaration, which emphasised both the unacceptable national and dynastic aspects of Union in Stuart eyes, while also obliquely acknowledging the 'bought and sold for English gold' Jacobite critique of that measure:

> With respect to the pretended Union of the two Nations, the king [i.e. James] cannot possibly ratify it, since he has had repeated Remonstrances against it from each Kingdom; and since it is incontestable, that the Principal Point then in View was the Exclusion of the Royal Family from their undoubted Right to the Crown, for which Purposes the Grossest Corruptions were openly used to bring it about.[5]

This was strong stuff, but in Edinburgh Charles was to some extent the prey of Scottish national feeling, and such explicit commitments acted as a salve to his support – though as a statement of Charles's own outlook, they may have been moderated, but not disowned. His conduct certainly shows a desire to win allies, even at a cost his restored father might well have found too dear: such perhaps was the reason for the Prince's declaration that he would 'secure' the established church in Scotland, a statement which might not have gone down well with his Episcopalian supporters. Feelings were certainly running high, and the nationalist commitment of Scottish Jacobites in Edinburgh was well displayed in the behaviour of James Hepburn of Keith:

> On the steps of Holyrood Palace, Hepburn of Keith . . . acted out a piece of theatre. He ostentatiously went ahead of the prince in a gallery touch meant to convey to the crowd both that Scotland took precedence over the House of Stuart and that to oppose Union with England was logically to be a Jacobite. (McLynn, 1988, 149)

Such sentiments almost imply a threatened degree of conditionality in Jacobite support, a nationalistic exaction of a price for supporting the native dynasty. This might be too emphatic a reading, for, as Michael Lynch says of the 1715 Rising, 'its motivation had been a close-knit mixture of traditional loyalty to an ancient monarchy and anti-Union feeling, which few as yet saw as other than indistinguishable' (Lynch, 1991, 328). Yet there are signs of a conditionality in Scottish Jacobite support. Lord Lovat, for example, who habitually played both sides in the dynastic quarrel, has been adjudged by one Jacobite historian as a man whose 'stalwart Scottish nationalism . . . was perhaps . . . [his] strongest emotion next to megalomania' (Lenman, 1984, 163). When Charles Edward came to Lovat's house after Culloden, his host urged him to 'Remember . . . your great ancestor Robert Bruce, who lost eleven battles and won Scotland by the twelfth'. In addition to such straightforwardly royalist iconography, there was the constitutional dimension which bound the Stuarts to support the restoration of the Estates, even had they been otherwise unwilling to do so. A 1707 memorial written within a week of the Union called for a Stuart restoration in Scotland alone (Gibson, 1988, 93–4), a position which remained (except possibly in 1708) a bridge too far for the Jacobite leadership. More remarkable, perhaps, was the 'serious plan to establish a republic in Scotland' examined among three other options by the French court in 1747. It was put forward by the Marquis d'Eguilles, who during the '45 had acted as ambassador to Charles Edward, and who had pled with him before Culloden not to give battle on such bad ground for his forces. The Marquis's suggestion, though ultimately impracticable, was evidence that there was at least one strand in French opinion which regarded the political aims of Scottish Jacobitism as just as important as the dynastic ones. Jacobites such as the Earl Marischal did, after all, eventually become republicans. Even the opinions of a Stuart loyalist such as Lochiel showed a strongly nationalist rather than dynastic bias after Culloden, when he hoped to 'deliver the kingdom of Scotland from the slavery to which it is, or will soon be, reduced'. There was thus some truth in the twentieth-century nationalist D. H. MacNeill's view that 'Jacobitism became a real force only in 1707 . . . in Scotland it was an essentially practical movement and not for Chairlie'. This book has argued for the veracity of the first part of this statement, in military terms at least.[6]

There are signs of the crucial importance of the Union in both the direction of Jacobite policy and also the actions of some Presbyterian nationalists. Several thousand burnt the articles of Union at Dumfries on 20 November 1706; in 1708, there were persistent rumours of there being Presbyterian forces ready to join a Jacobite rising. Ker of Kersland's double-dealing and failure to produce Cameronian Jacobite troops did not altogether dampen Jacobite hopes of wooing these extreme Presbyterians to the Stuart standard. George Lockhart of Carnwath, one of the few Jacobite leaders who lived in Covenanting territory, considered that the opposition of certain strands in Presbyterian opinion towards Union was so great that it could push them into the Jacobite camp. They argued, he wrote, that 'God may convert him [James], or he may have Protestant children, but the Union can never be good'. Lockhart stuck to this view of Jacobite potential among the Presbyterians over many years, as is clear from a letter he wrote to the Earl Marischal in April 1719 (though Lockhart's categorisation of the sympathies of the western Presbyterians is not quite so clear):

> Tho the King [James] does not want some friends in the western shires, yet the gross of the people, both gentry and commons, are either prysbyterians [sic] favourably disposed towards the present Government, or pritty indifferent as to all Governments whatsoever. But as the far greatest part of both have an heartie aversion to the Union, if once they were convinced that the King's prosperity would terminate in the dissolution therof, there is reason to believe a great many of the first would be converted, at least so far as to be neutral, and most of the others declare for him . . . the Earl Marischal should . . . declare that it is the King's intention to restore his Scots subjects to their ancient rights and independent state. And that he and those with him appear in arms as well to redeem the nation as restore the King.

'As well to redeem the nation as restore the king': this phrase indicated the equipoise between nationalism and royalism for ideological Jacobites such as Lockhart, whose deep antipathy to the Union is clear enough from his 'Memoirs' and actions in public business in both the Scottish and British parliaments.[7]

James attempted for some time to woo the Cameronians, in the hope that they would join forces with more conventional Jacobites to effect his restoration. As Lockhart supposed advisable, the king's plea was centred on anti-Union feeling, as in this letter of 31 October 1718, signed by Mar:

> Whereas we are certainly informed that it hath pleased
> Almighty God so to touch the heart of many of our people in
> Scotland, commonly called Cameronians, with a sense of their
> duty to us and their native country, that they are ready to join
> in any undertaking which shall tend by force of arms to
> restore us to the throne of our ancestors, and our kingdom of
> Scotland to its ancient free and independent state . . . There-
> fore, that nothing reasonable may be wanting on our part . . .
> we hereby renew the promises we have already made in our
> former declaration, in relation to the unhappy union of our
> two kingdoms, which we thereby declared null and void from
> the beginning.

Although duty to the House of Stuart is named first as a cause for
taking arms in this appeal for support, it is clear from the emphasis
on it in this declaration that the Union is the major issue by reason
of which the Jacobite leadership hopes for Cameronian help.[8]

If extreme Covenanting opinion was hard to woo to the Stuart
side except in the immediate aftermath of Union, there was ample
success elsewhere. The size of the army which flocked to Mar in
1715, far larger than any royalist force in the previous century, bore
material witness to the strength of anti-Union feeling. Mar, who
had supported the measure in 1707, made an issue of his opposition
to Union eight years later, while James's own declaration of 15
October 1714 (perhaps that which is referred to in the message to
the Cameronians above) cannot have failed to provide encouragement to those of like views. It stated that he would

> relieve our Subjects of Scotland, from the hardships they
> groan under on account of the late unhappy Union, and to
> restore the Kingdom to its ancient free and independent state
> . . . We hope . . . to see our just Rights, and those of the
> Church and People of Scotland once more settled in a free and
> independent Scots Parliament, on their Ancient Foundation.

James's description of Scotland as 'my own ancient kingdom', and
the nature of Mar's approaches to those who might be interested in
joining the Rising had a distinctively nationalist tone. Even after the

indecisive (but ultimately fatal) encounter at Sheriffmuir, Mar's proposed Association at Perth aimed to 'Never . . . admit of Terms till the King was restored, the Union broken and the Church established' (Taylers, 1936, 116). The standard raised at Braemar (or by Viscount Kenmure in the south) bore on one side the Scottish arms in gold, on the other the thistle with the motto *Nemo me impune lacessit* and the words 'No Union'. Mar ordered 'all the towns to pay the taxes and duties only on the old Scots footing'; both in 1715 and thirty years later (with regard to the hated malt tax), the promise of lower taxes in an independent Scotland formed a powerful propaganda weapon for supporters of the Stuarts (it had in fact been the 1713 attempt to introduce the malt tax to Scotland which had led to an attempt to overturn Union in the Lords (Lynch, 1991, 322)). In 1745, the Jacobite broadswords were to carry the legend 'Prosperity to Scotland and no Union'. Both risings thus bore witness to the national dimension in Scottish Jacobitism: the 'honourable and beautifull' duty of resistance from the Scots Nation (against British sovereignty), in the words of the Master of Sinclair.[9]

The Episcopal Church was a major engine of anti-Union feeling. It was no accident that its restoration formed the third demand of Mar's Association, or that a Jacobite ideologue such as Lockhart should have a central say in the nomination of its bishops. The central Scottishness of the Episcopal communion in the early eighteenth century belies its later miscalling as the 'English' church; but, for all that, it was possessed of a strongly British ecclesiastical dimension, borne out not only by its historic links with the Laudian church but also by its more recent ones with the English Nonjurors. To sum up, perhaps over-simplistically, the paradox of the Scottish church, Episcopalians were political nationalists and ecclesiastical unionists, while the established Presbyterian Kirk was the reverse.

Just as was the case with Stuart opposition to the Union, the Episcopal Church had another motive for disliking it besides straightforward nationalism. The Stuart royal family viewed the Union as a confirmation of the Act of Settlement, specifically designed to reinforce their exclusion; the Episcopalians could in a similar light see it as confirming the domination of Presbyterianism, now guaranteed the rights of an established church in perpetuity on the back of an earlier coup, when

> The General Assembly which met in November 1690 was not as general as it might have been; only 180 ministers and elders attended, all from south of the Tay. In effect, it was a partition church of southern Scotland which claimed the right to deprive all ministers who fell short of its ideal of full-blown presbyterianism. (Lynch, 304)

The endorsement of such a rebuff in 1707 was all the more galling because it had been passed by an English Anglican Parliament, whose own established church was the normal natural ally of the Scottish Episcopal interest. The Nonjuring and certain High Church Anglicans (who in 1712 helped give toleration to those Episcopalians who would acknowledge the reigning monarch) were sympathetic, but, as time went on, jurant Anglicanism and Episcopalianism grew further apart. The tendency of even High Church Anglicans who took the oaths towards Jacobitism cannot have hindered attempts to turn the Church of England into the Hanoverian regime at prayer: half a decade after the 1722 Jacobite plot associated with the name of Francis Atterbury, Bishop of Rochester, all the bench of bishops were Whigs. In such circumstances, the only partners whom the Episcopalian church could find south of the border were the English Nonjurors, in whose movement the Scottish church played a disproportionately important role, owing to the fact that a far larger portion of the Scottish than the English clergy had refused to accept the new regime in 1688–9. Indeed, in 1777, due to diminishing numbers of English adherents, the Nonjuror Bishop Gordon gave his flock into the care of the Scottish Episcopal Church, which six years later became the mother church of the American Episcopal church through the consecration of Bishop Seabury in what is now the main quadrangle of Marischal College in Aberdeen.[10]

Episcopalian opposition to Union was in no contradiction to their close links with the English Nonjurors. The Episcopalians believed that only by ending the Union could a proper ecclesiastical settlement be restored to Scotland, because the Union entrenched Presbyterian rights; the Nonjurors saw the restoration of the Stuarts as the only route back to a caesaro-sacramentalist monarchy. This was, in the Jacobite Thomas Cappoch's words, 'the Church of England, as she stood before the Revolution, which I firmly believe to be truly primitive, Catholic and Apostolic': the 'British Catholic' dimension of the Nonjurors and attempts to seek union with the Orthodox were aspects of nonjurant Anglicanism which indicated the extent of its divergence from Hanoverian Lutheranism and the juring Church of England. Such a church as Cappoch and his ideological fellow-travellers spoke of could only be fitly governed by a Stuart monarchy, and such a monarchy would also restore the Scottish Episcopal Church to its rights, in so doing abrogating a Union intended to exclude both a caesaro-sacramentalist monarchy and the church that supported it. The Union itself was, on this reading, only one in a catalogue of disasters which had attended Scotland's disobedience to its ancient native line of kings, from the famine of the 1690s through the collapse of the Darien scheme and the Hanoverian succession. Such disasters were the inevitable price of disobedience to the caesaro-sacramentalist monarch. Episcopalian ideologues showed awareness of the link between monarchy, church and Union, as did Professor James Garden in a sermon preached 'in the New Church of Aberdeen' during the 1715 Rising:

> By it [the Revolution] the ancient Apostolick Form of Church Government was abolished . . . the Rights of the Church usurped by Schismatical Teachers, who have set up a Seperate [sic] Communion from the Catholick Church of Christ in all ages . . . For thes [sic] heinous Sins and Abominations of Rebellion, Injustice, Oppression, Schism and perjury, God in his just wrath hath visited and plagued us with a long, a bloody and expensive war, several years of famine and extraordinary Dearth, accompany'd with Epidemical diseases and a great Mortality, whereby the wealth and strength of this nation has been exhausted and our land in a great measure dispeopled: with the loss of the Liberty, privileges and independency of this our Ancient Kingdom: with bondage under a forraign prince . . . the only natural and

proper remedy . . . the Restauration of his present Matie [Majesty], James the 8th.

Garden goes on to say that the Presbyterians have

allowed and tamely permitted the Nation basely and shame-fully to be sold and enslaved contrary to the Express Remon-strances of most part of the Kingdom, under the specious name and pretence of an Union with England.

The Union is thus one of the catastrophes which has followed as a result of national disobedience to the monarchy and established church. Moreover, the Presbyterians have betrayed the trust reposed in them as the new established church by collaborating in selling the kingdom into slavery. Presbyterian dominance is linked with the loss of national liberty (as indeed had been the case under Cromwell), Episcopacy with that liberty restored. In such circum-stances it is not surprising that, as P. W. J. Riley points out, 'many [anti-union] addresses were signed by people who had refused the oaths [i.e. mainly Episcopalians and Catholics], thus equating them with disaffection'. To be disaffected from the Union was to support Jacobite ecclesiastical and political policy, at the core of which lay, ever more markedly as time went on, the confessional issue (Riley, 1978, 282). Indeed, many anti-Union Episcopal clergy left for the colonies under financial and political pressure: 'the Reverend Alexander Garden, for example, emigrated to Charleston South Carolina around 1720 and he died there in 1756' (Lenman, 1984, 211).[11]

In the Episcopalian pursuit of the restoration of Scottish national liberty, the Stuart monarchy continued to be important. The church was bound to the dynasty not only because it had always been favoured by them, but also perhaps due to Episco-palian history's dwelling on the ancient antecedents of the Scottish royal line, and the early history of the country in general. As Colin Kidd observes, 'Jacobites were in fact far better able to exploit the history of Scotland's imperial crown than whigs' (Kidd, 1993, 74), and this extended to the Gaeltachd, where Margaret Campbell saw the tartan as an 'immemorial Scottish custom "since King

Fergus was crowned"'. Such sentiments go far to endorse the link between the patriot Highlander motif and the Jacobites who developed it, for Highland dress is seen by Margaret Campbell to be as aboriginally Scottish as the Stuart dynasty itself (though this sentiment is not strictly Episcopalian property). The pro-Stuart apologetics of such figures as Sir George Mackenzie, James VII and II's Lord Advocate, used Scotland's real and traditional early history in a manner which would not have been acceptable to many Presbyterian writers. The Stuart monarchs echoed these apologetics. In the 1684 Holyrood portraits, inheritance and 'sequencing' had both been important in a display 'culminating in the Stewarts', while sixty years later the centrality of the Stuart dynasty to the Scottish royal line and by implication the historic (and therefore genuine) national identity of Scotland continued to be borne witness to. In 1743, King James declared that 'Our Progenitors have swayed the Sceptre with Glory, through a longer Succession of Kings, than any Monarchy upon Earth can at this Day boast of': in this context, perhaps Hawley's dragoons acted with an acute insight into political symbolism in taking 'sabres to the paintings' at Holyrood in 1746. Despite their explosion by eighteenth-century (ironically sometimes Jacobite) scholarship, such statements of foundation history were important for a patriotic reading of the Scottish past, for 'the ancient line of kings supplied a vital counterweight to an English historiographical tradition which insisted that Scotland was and always had been a dependency of the crown of England'.[12] Presbyterian apologists, on the other hand, often found themselves in difficulty when dealing with the struggles for independence in the Middle Ages, or the ancient rights of the Scottish crown, as this was a period when 'dismal darkness did remain / and overspread the nation'. Despite efforts to capture the Celtic Culdee church for Presbyterian ideology, the belief of such writers tended to be that *their* glorious Reformation marked a new beginning. Episcopalian writers and those who sympathised with them had, by contrast, greater freedom in their ability to use the past as evidence for a long history of Scottish struggles for liberty. In the continuation of such struggles, the exiled monarch, now suffering and starved of his right, was a partner for the abandoned nation.

The loyal address of the Episcopalian clergy of 'your antient kingdom of Scotland' to James on 29 December 1715 makes this point in stating that 'Almighty God has been pleased to train up your Majesty from your infancy in the school of the Cross' (Taylers, 1936, 130). James was in a sense the 'Suffering Servant', whose restoration alone could end 'the fatal union of the 2 kingdoms', by renewing health and fertility in the Scottish polity. Thus it was that in both the risings of 1715 and 1745 the Episcopalian 'clergy were leaders, and the army . . . was recruited from their congregations'.[13]

In return for this support, the Stuarts continued to offer their backing to a church of which they were not members. James nominated Episcopalian and Anglican Nonjuring bishops, and was even prepared to back his Scottish agents such as Lockhart in their attempts to support traditional Episcopalian doctrines against the Catholicising practices of the Usagers. In England, James was prepared to defend Anglican theological claims, writing in a letter of 29 November 1717 from Urbino (mainly concerning Benjamin Hoadley, who had been elevated to the see of Bangor in December 1715) of the 'Intrinsic spiritual power of the Church or power of the Keys . . . [which] hath ever been thought an Essential right of the Church of England'. In England, the Nonjurors were left largely alone unless they participated in armed insurrection or major plots, but in Scotland, the national dimension and claims of disestablished Episcopalianism led to military action on the part of the authorities as early as 1711, while in 1716 'militia and dragoons' were 'used against Episcopalian congregations' in the north-east. The militant and nationalist Jacobite dimension of the Episcopalians rendered them a more potent threat. Unity was, however, of great importance in maintaining the integrity of such Scottish patriotism, and here the Episcopalians were not always more successful than their Nonjuring brethren, who suffered frequent schism. In 1724, for example, Lockhart feared that a dispute between the bishops might lead to 'the loss of the common cause in these loyal shyres [Angus and Mearns]'. The security of the Episcopalian communion was fragile, but it was that communion which bonded a continuing Scottish patriotism with the 'Privileges . . . maintain'd by our Heroick ancestors', ancestors whose religious convictions were often an embarrassment to Presbyterianism. Thus Lockhart of Carnwath was simultaneously a business manager for James's ecclesiastical appointments and a persistent agitator for 'a declaration for Scotland bruiting the dissolution of the Union', as he wrote in a letter of 25 January 1726.[14]

Not all Episcopalians were as sure of their ground as was Lockhart in his unstinting Jacobitism. The failure of the Stuarts to regain their thrones might be seen as a sign of a change in divine attitude towards their claims: indeed, Williamite Tories had begun to espouse this view by 1700. More surprising is the presence of such views in the writing of committed Jacobites. Alexander Forbes, 4th Lord Pitsligo, is usually thought of as one of the most uncompromising ideological Jacobites of all: out in both the '15 and the '45, he was in hiding for sixteen years after serving as General of Horse in the latter Rising. Yet far from being an unreconstructed ideologue of indefeasible right, Pitsligo offers a window into a much more complex realm of interior debate than his actions might seem to indicate. In two MS memoranda, ' On Government' and 'A letter on Governments' written around 1720 (which may be first and second drafts of a study he did not complete), Pitsligo moves towards an argument for government's drawing on consent for its legitimacy which is not far removed from an extreme Whig contractual position. Although the power of Providence retains a strong position in Lord Forbes's arguments, the ideas that 'the benefit and *good of the governed*' is '*the only end [design* inserted] *of Government*', and 'whatever hands it may be put in . . . It is not to be considered a patrimonial esteat or property of the Governor', sound unexpectedly democratic from what is predicated of Jacobite behaviour from a traditional point of view. Pitsligo seems to accept the need for 'submission to . . . new Governments when Providence has once settled them', and, in his later and better-known 1745 Apologia, takes the trouble to explain why he nevertheless came out in the Rising of that year: though 'it might be thought a wicked thing to disturb a settled government, and involve the Country in Civil War', there were nevertheless sufficient protests and resentments against Hanover to suggest that the consent of the people had been withdrawn. Although Lord Forbes to some extent seems to shift his ground towards a more straightforwardly Jacobite position in this Apologia, he remains aware of the importance of consistency, and discusses the '45 in terms of the circumstances of the time which, Pitsligo believes, set it apart:

> Considering some strong parliamentary speeches and the general cry without doors against standing armies, arbitrary government, foreign dominions to which the blood and treasure of Britain are sacrificed in a shameful manner and our condition growing daily more desperate, as the hardships go on in a regular parliamentary way.
>
> To expel this poison, I and others of more consequence took arms in the year 1745.

It is interesting to note that Lord Forbes, himself a firm opponent of Union, talks here in terms of British patriotism. One of the tasks of a restored Stuart monarchy in London would be to fulfil its ancient duties by restoring the Estates; but this might well be without prejudice to a wider Britain of separate realms but common aims. Pitsligo's thought is of interest by reason both of its uncertainty and complexity: it shows that Episcopalian ideologues could be more desirous of true argument than righteous assertion.[15]

Episcopalianism's survival as an agent for Jacobite nationalism was finally confronted by Cumberland in 1746, when Episcopalian chapels throughout the north and north-east were burnt, particularly in Moray and Ross, where the church was strongest. The penal legislation which followed had the twofold effect of outlawing Scottish orders and ensuring the significant presence of an increasing number of licensed English clergy in jurant Anglican orders to minister in Scotland. Such men not only owed their livings to the downgraded status of the church; they were, and were no doubt designed to be by origin and politics, less sympathetic to the Scottish agenda at the heart of Episcopalian ideology.[16]

Licensed clergy of this kind had begun to minister in Scotland after 1715, under the supervision of English and Irish bishops. Following the penal legislation of 1747, their numbers naturally increased, and the native church was reduced to the brink of extinction, despite the fact that, as in the case of Catholicism, the penal laws appear to have been so strict as to be seldom applied in full vigour. In 1689, there had been 607 Scottish Episcopalian clergy. By 1731, that number had fallen to 125. Not long after Culloden, 'when its cup of suffering was full, only four bishops and forty-two priests remained where one hundred years before fourteen bishops and archbishops and a thousand priests had ministered'. Even at this stage, however, there could be congregations up to 800 strong, and no doubt a proportion of continuing Jacobite unrest in the towns can be attributed to those who remained loyal to a communion which did not separate from its allegiance to the Stuarts until 1788, though even then a few diehards clung onto Jacobitism, including the Bishop of Dunblane. No doubt such activity helped to ensure that 'the clergy of the Episcopal church were still debarred by statute from officiating for a single day in the Church of England till 1840' (Perry, 1933, 37). By then, the native church had reached a *modus vivendi* with licensed Anglicanism in Scotland which still obtains, and has helped to give the Episcopalian church the character which it now possesses. The church finally joined the Anglican Communion in 1867, and during the nineteenth century it was a descendant of the Jacobite Lord Forbes of Pitsligo who helped to work towards 'the . . . hope of reunion with the Roman section of Christendom', as well as doing much to re-establish the church in general (Perry, 76). His ancestor, who 'though sincerely attached to his own Communion . . . avoided in himself, and duly reprobated in others, any unkindness of feeling towards those of an opposite form or system', would doubtless have approved, although such moves were opposed by the restored Roman Catholic hierarchy in England.[17]

The Stuart dynasty's own interests and those of the Episcopal Church in Scotland were thus at one in rejecting the Union settlement, an action taken on the basis of principle in the second case, and possibly in the first: certainly, whatever, the advantages of expediency, Stuart opposition to Union did not waver significantly. But what of the Scots below the level of the ideological leadership provided by Church and King? Bruce Lenman has argued that political consciousness did not effectively exist below the level of the gentry in the Jacobite period; and, vexed as this question undoubtedly is, work carried out on English Jacobitism by Paul Monod and others casts doubt on whether this was the case. In Scottish terms, the profile of the urban volunteers cited in Chapter 2 may also suggest a popular Jacobitism; so too do some of the manifestations of Jacobite culture. Whereas artefacts such as glassware were more the preserve of a high cultural market, there is ample evidence that Jacobite literature contained a political critique of Whig power – and that such critiques were altered, adapted and adjusted in folk culture we know from work on both Scottish and Irish songs.[18]

The Episcopal clergy themselves participated in the culture of their congregations, not only in compositions such as John Skinner's 'Tullochgorum', but also as gestures of Jacobite defiance. The Reverend Mr Troup of Muchalls, imprisoned in Stonehaven Jail after the '45, played Jacobite airs such as 'O'er the water to Charlie', 'Sow's tail to Geordie' and 'Bonnie Charlie's noo awa' daily (saving Sunday!) on the pipes. Those sympathetic to their cause such as William Hamilton of Bangour (who fought in the '45) and Robert Fergusson also linked high and folk cultural literary tastes, Fergusson's classicising 'Edina' being counterbalanced by his enthusiasm for Scottish traditional music. Both poets strongly linked their Jacobitism to anti-Unionism: Hamilton of Bangour wrote of the '45 as straight Anglo-Scottish conflict:

> If thee, *O Scotland*, I forget,
> Even with my latest Breath;
> May foul Dishonour stain my Name,
> And bring a Coward's Death . . .
> Remember *England's* Children, Lord,
> Who, on *Drumossie* Day,
> Deaf to the Voice of kindred Love
> 'Raze, raze it quite', did say.

Such sentiments are noteworthy not so much for their accuracy as for what they tell us about the construction of Scottish Jacobite ideology.[19]

If such writers could not be accounted properly part of folk culture, this was not true of the balladeers and hawkers who formed such an important part of cultural interchange in a century where written versions of songs were already interpenetrating with oral culture. In 1716, there was 'an epidemic of Jacobite ballad-hawking', while 'the street ballad-singers were irrepressible'. Their use of popular airs to a seditious set (as in the case of 'The Piper o' Dundee', discussed above) gave 'no handle to the law officers of the Crown'. According to government intelligence, clergy used the Jacobite lyric as a means of stirring up disaffection: one report specifically mentions 'songs put into their hands by the Priests . . . these & severale [sic] Rebellious & Scurrilous pieces printed in the years 1716 & 1746'. What was the content of such songs, and how widely did they circulate?[20]

Recently, more (though arguably not enough) has been written on the Jacobite song. In 1989, the present author suggested that such songs might be appropriately divided into three types, each dealing with a major theme: the romantic, the sacred and the active/aggressive. Songs which attack the Union are common in all three of these categories. One of the pirated versions of *Auld Lang Syne*, entitled *The true Scots Mens Lament for the Loss of the Rights of their Ancient Kingdom*, strongly associated the loss of the Stuarts and respect for antiquity with the end of Scottish independence, while the versified version of 'Belhaven's Vision' (a deliberately populist national appeal from Lord Belhaven in the last Scottish Parliament) was designed for popular currency. It too concentrated on ancestors and a betrayal of antiquity, naming both the legendary heroes and famous families of a past Scotland: '*Fergus . . . Stewarts . . . Gordons . . . Murrays . . . Grahams*' who 'For Freedom stood'. Both poems concentrated on the selling of Scottish independence, for Imperial trade ('Tobacco') and the 'little shining Clay' of English bribery respectively.[21]

The 'Highland Laddie' song-cycle in which the Highlander-as-patriot tradition was partly contained also gave vent to specifically Scottish national feeling, not only in 'My Love He Was a Highland Lad' (quoted above in Chapter 1), but also in songs such as 'The True Scotsmans Lamentation' (even the title is distinctly indicative of its sympathies):

When Southward I do set my Face
And cast my Eyes on Edinburgh
I cannot look upon that Place
But straight it strikes my heart with Sorrow
To see a house stand empty now
Where men had wont to be right gaudy . . .

The empty city is emptied both of its sovereignty and its 'Bonie bonie Highland Laddie', who emblemises and can restore it. It was a commonplace of Jacobite poetry that the loss of 'The Stuarts' ancient freeborn race' was linked to the fact that 'Scotland and England must be now / United in a nation', as 'The Curses' put it; and insofar as the Union was the main means of extending the Act of Settlement to Scotland, this was by no means too far wide of the mark. The Scottish past and its monarchs were fondly remembered, as was the Auld Alliance: 'Why did you thy Union break / thou had of late [under Mary] with *France*?', as one song put it – though, as outlined in Chapter 1, such sentiments might well be damaging insofar as they served Hanoverian British xenophobia.[22]

It is clear that such songs had a wide circulation. Not only is there the evidence of government reports on recruiting for the Irish Brigades; there is also the long-standing tradition of the subversive use of balladeers. In the sixteenth century, the Catholic authorities in Scotland had tried to suppress such hawkers because of the Protestant material they circulated; in the seventeenth, the Cromwellian administration in Ireland took similar action because of the widespread diffusion of oppositional sentiments through this class, who were after all primary carriers of news in a largely immobile culture with a still strong oral tradition (in Gaelic Jacobite verse, 'the vast majority of the poems . . . have been preserved at some stage by oral transmission'). The importance of these singing men in eighteenth-century Jacobitism is attested to not only in the 400 or 500 broadsides routinely dished out to balladeers by English Jacobite propagandists such as Francis Clifton, but also in the distribution of 'Jacobite medals, prints and portraits' by smugglers and the presence of such singing men in Jacobite armies. 'The

Chevalier's Muster-Roll' ('Little wot ye wha's coming') was apparently composed on 12 November 1715 for Mackintosh of Borlum's
brigade on their march south: appropriately for sentiments of
Jacobite unity, it was a song in English to be accompanied by a
(presumably Gaelic-speaking) Highland piper. One impertinent
balladeer even claimed to be 'Ballad-Singer in Ordinary in Great
Britain' to King James. Not only was the material of such people
sung or its air played and the words passed out in broadside form;
it appears (particularly in safe areas) that the balladeers used that
ancient nexus of folk culture, the ale-house, as a safe place to post
up their seditious words. Even the older Border ballad tradition
was brought into play, as when the set of 'Chevy Chase' was 'sung
to the air of "Derwentwater's Farewell"': the Anglo-Scottish conflict of an earlier age became transposed into the present, as was
later to be the case in the repertoire of Agnes Lyle. Indeed, Derwentwater was generally Scotticised in the ballads, such as 'Lord
Dunwaters', which grew up about him, thus rendering the Jacobite
conflict in over-simplified Anglo-Scottish terms. That these terms
were embodied in folk culture perhaps tells us something of the
underlying specifically Scottish patriotism in Jacobite culture, as
'Let our brave loyal clans' puts it:

> All unions we'll o'erturn, boys,
> Which caus'd our nation mourn, boys,
> Like Bruce at Bannockburn, boys,
> The English home we'll chase.

The use of Bruce and Wallace as loyalist motifs of Scottish patriotism has been discussed elsewhere, and they are recalled in the
Buchan Jacobite song, 'Wha wadna fecht for Charlie':

> Think on Scotia's ancient heroes
> Think on foreign foes repelled
> Think on glorious Bruce and Wallace . . .[23]

'Ancient heroes' were central to the messianic qualities of Jacobite
poetic argument, the idea that the returning monarch would trans-
form the land:

All Beasts that go upon all Four
Go leap and dance around;
Because that the curst Union's broke,
And fallen to the ground.

Union here becomes a metaphorical tree of bondage, which is broken by the returning Stuart: the imagery of such writing is very close to that of Gaelic writers who continued to believe that 'the just king's reign was accompanied by plenitude and fine weather, while storms and poverty were signs of something rotten in the state'. In this mood, Alexander MacDonald (Alasdair MacMhaighstir Alasdair) 'found a way to fuse together his vision of the Stuarts, of Gaeldom, and of an ideal Scotland'. The idealisation of the Stuart monarchy was so intense in Jacobite propaganda precisely because it was a function of the idealisation of the nation itself and its potential, an idealisation largely carried out in terms of the cultural representations with which Scottish Episcopalianism and Catholicism were more comfortable than were at least the more dedicated adherents of the established Kirk. The nationalism of Jacobitism gave it much of its strength in both images and recruits when it was a viable political option; afterwards, the romanticisation of Jacobitism consigned both it and the nationalism to which it was so intimately related to the margin of heritage. Before 1760, nationalism gave Jacobitism its strength; after 1790, Jacobitism, or more correctly the romantic misreading of Jacobitism, drained nationalism of its relevance. In *The Invention of Scotland* (1991), I outlined the development of this process. The last chapter in this study examines the presentation of the heritage of romance through kitsch, and the controlling role which such presentation can play in manipulating a cultural response.[24]

CHAPTER 4

Kitsch in Culture

Kitsch may be defined as elaborately aestheticized commodities produced in the name of large institutions (church, state, empire, monarchy) for middle-class home use. Kitsch is in short charisma, charisma that has obviously been recently manufactured.

Thomas Richards

Come on in . . . and experience Prince Charlie's Scottish Extravaganza a colourful blend of Food, Music, Song and Dance in the Royal Mile's most attractive setting. Following a complimentary drink in our Highland Dress Exhibition area, your evening begins as our piper, resplendent in Full Highland Dress, leads you into the Great Hall . . . The Prince's story unfolds in our magnificent setting . . . with . . . our own special version of Prince Charles Edward Stuart tartan . . . the combination . . . creates a Wonderful Jacobean [sic] Ambience!

The Scottish Experience, 12 High Street, Edinburgh

The Scottish Tartans Museum at Comrie in Perthshire has acquired a reputation as a quasi-official authority on the Garb of Old Gaul. The Piping Heritage Centre at Dunvegan in Skye . . . peddles the myth of the MacCrimmon musical dynasty beside which the Bachs pale into insignificance. The Highland Tryst Museum in Crieff portrays that douce little burgh as a sort of Dodge City in the rain, the 'capital of royal Strathearn, wild frontier town where Highlands met Lowlands . . . '. And it is interesting that while there are five clan museums and heritage centres . . . there are no museums charting the history of fearsome border tribes like the Armstrongs, the Kerrs or the Elliots.

George Rosie

The tone of much older Scottish history (as well as some new) is uncomfortably certain and too assured to be true.

Ian Donnachie and Christopher Whatley[1]

This book began with an examination of the enduring quality of popular (and indeed scholarly) misrepresentations of Jacobitism, which centre on the Myth of the Jacobite Clans. Whether a romantic or sceptical reading of this myth is purveyed, the end result is the same: the presentation of Jacobitism as of marginal importance in the continuing narrative of British history. By that very token, however, it becomes more emphatically a part of that world we have lost that is so dear to the marketing pretensions of heritage, a term defined in the Introduction. Moreover, Jacobitism is one of the very earliest subjects to receive treatment as heritage. In the romantic and pageant-ridden zone of the early nineteenth century, when the conduct of the Highlanders in the Napoleonic Wars had valorised the heroic Celt to an unequalled degree, the rehabilitation of Jacobitism was an important factor in sustaining the Highland cult (it must not be forgotten that this cult was developing at the same time as some of the major Clearances were taking place, so divorced was jacobitised Highlandism from continuing history). In Colin Kidd's words, 'By applying a sentimental Jacobite gloss to a basic Whig constitutionalism, Scott turned the Scottish past into an ideologically neutral pageant . . .' (1994, 7). Scott of course was not wholly to blame, but his 'tableau of extinct heroics' was certainly seductive and colourful. The Jacobite past was in some terms a tissue of papist intrigue and misplaced loyalties: discarding the first (which in any case could be seen as the international, as opposed to the native Scoto-British dimension), the second could serve as a token of the future military fidelity of Scotland to the British government. It was no coincidence that the production of tartan increased to a great degree at the time of the 1822 visit, rather as in more seriously Jacobite days the price of white roses had rocketed in London in 1716. When the *Edinburgh Observer* announced that 'We are all now Jacobites . . . in acknowledging George IV', it was endorsing a semantic and symbolic shift in the definition of the term, which simultaneously sealed its old meaning in obsolescence by covering it in the glamour of sentiment while celebrating a rebirth of Jacobite spirit in the unity and pluck of British imperial success and loyalty to the crown in the face of Jacobinism and Bonapartism. Since 1789, the French had finally proved as untrustworthy as every true Briton had always guessed them to be: the central supporters of historic Jacobitism had shown their contempt for dynastic rights by getting rid of kings altogether. Just as emigrant Jacobite clansmen had fought on George III's side in the American Revolution, so now it was the duty of those who had been Stuart loyalists to protect the monarchy itself. The restoration of the lands or titles of the Jacobite nobility, begun in the 1780s and extended in the decades following 1820, reinforced the shifting terms of political loyalty: the place in society was regained, but it now indicated something else, a signified fidelity to the new monarchy which had graciously reinstated it. In an imperial age, that fidelity was centrally military. The tartan was now an icon of a faithful and unifying, not a treacherous and divisive, resort to arms.[2]

It is that military fidelity which is surely the key to the power of jacobitical kitsch (a word which means 'to put together sloppily': an apt description for some popular Jacobite history). From the pageantry of Sir Walter Scott onwards, the (ancestrally Jacobite) Highlander is often presented in military garb. The tartan itself, so insistently used and criticised as a symbol of Scottish identity, was only accepted as legitimate wear in Britain for military use almost half a century after the '45. Tartan's symbolic link with (militant) Jacobitism in the first half of the eighteenth century became transformed into its status as a solely military dress in the latter half. The tartan of civil threat became the tartan of imperial triumph, as battle honours accrued to Scottish troops who were often used recklessly to gain them. Tartan was the indicator of loyalty and the means whereby a putatively misplaced Jacobite loyalty was transmuted into the true loyalty to Great Britain and her role in the world. For a long time, the only means whereby this could be done were military ones: after all, at the same time as Highland troops were gaining credit and casualties in the Seven Years' War, Bute and other Scots were being depicted in tartan as dangerous Jacobites by the Wilkesites and their fellow-travellers. Anti-Scottishness in British civil society remained so strong that even a man at the top of the tree like Dundas could, in 1778 and while drinking in English company, break 'out into an invective against the English', saying 'he would move for a repeal of the Union'. Nor was this an isolated incident: one Scottish resident of London wrote in 1763 that 'if the English are to be treated as sons, but the Scots as step-sons, by the King . . . then let the Union be dissolved'. The tartanised Scot was still for many years a suspected alien at home: hence that the symbolic importance placed on tartan's positive military associations was enduring should come as no surprise.[3]

The link between tartanry and the '45 has also quite often remained explicit, on the level of the heritage experiences cited above as well as in the more mundane area of Scottish product lines ('Claymore' whisky and 'Highlander – the Crisp of the Clans' are only two of the most recent). The Jacobitism thus depicted is both wholly Highland and wholly sanitised, both features being a part of the process of elaborate aestheticisation postulated in Richards's definition of kitsch. A Highland Jacobitism reinforces an aesthetic of military loyalty which is also colourful and concentrated, ironing out both the religious and international elements of Jacobitism, and presenting a selective and seemingly consciously romanticised picture of its national dimension. This is a provincialising process which creates 'the lure of witnessing an unadulterated, insular tradition as practised by simple pastoral innocents: a key impetus to the very worst condescensions in tourism'.[4] At the same time, such condescension is made bearable by the fact that it contains a degree of envy valorised (to take one dimension as an example), by the superior strength and masculinity of the heroic primitive male. As Carolyn Williams has recently argued, the Jacobite Highlander has been acculturated to British identity not only in simply military but also in heavily masculinised terms. Despite the fact that the Jacobite forces were on the whole composed of rather small men (around 5' 5"), and that (as we have seen), these men were on the whole quite ordinary individuals with ordinary livelihoods, they have from an early date been subject to various processes of hyperbole. The Highlandisation of the Jacobite army served to alienise it as not only strange and terrible, but also by that token sublime (like their landscapes) and fearsomely masculine. The chivalry, loyalty and savagery of the constructed Jacobite Highlander alike served to emphasise his subscription to a male world which was being elegised by the time of the Romantic period: for example, in Edmund Burke's celebrated passage on the beautiful and pathetic Marie Antoinette, now at the mercy of cruel revolutionists because of France's abandonment of the sublime practices of nobility and chivalry (and Burke himself was of course one of the foremost theorists of the sublime). The 'sophisters and oeconomists' of a new age liked, like Scott, to imagine themselves heroes in the sublime and departed world of the Highlands. So, what had (while Jacobitism had still been a threat) been the hyperbole of cannibalism and brutal savagery became subtly transmuted into one of an authentic and positive primitive loyalty, size and strength. The portrait photographs and other depictions of big Highland soldiers in the Victorian period thus became part of a process which continues, as Williams points out, right into the commercial iconography of the Crisp of the Clans and Scott's Porage Oats. The rippling muscles of the handsome Highland porridge-eater set off his crisp constrained features. From cannibalism to porridge is a big dietary shift, but the special qualities of the Highland warrior male are maintained throughout, albeit in increasingly sanitised terms – a process of sanitisation which begins with incorporation into the British military machine, and proceeds to the commercial exploitation of the glamour and strength which those nostalgic for more colourful days have felt since at least the Romantic period.[5]

The process whereby any bloodiness or conflict is sanitised away is also found in the more explicit iconography of Jacobitism, particularly in the symbolic choice of innocent and boyish depictions of its most famous leader: the cherubic pictures of Charles Edward Stuart which so often stand as misleading synecdoches for the Jacobite movement are surely chosen as a symbols because of the way they facilitate a cleansing retreat into nostalgia. In the image of his uncomplicated youth, the Prince provides an apparent innocent simplicity in which the role of partial and misrepresenting romance may sport at will. If one even counts the number of books on the cause which use such images of a betartaned Prince on the cover, it is clear how important a marketing tool such aestheticised Jacobitism is. The level of historical importance attained by the Year of the Prince is itself a product of Charles's charisma; his retention as the central figure of Jacobite heroism and endeavour by kitsch should thus not surprise, for kitsch depends very powerfully on the reproduction of charisma for its market appeal.[6]

But it is more than that, as Richards's definition of kitsch also indicates. If kitsch is primarily a popular expression of the great institutions of state made through mass material culture (as in Coronation mugs, picture postcards, photographic sequences of the Princesses Elizabeth and Margaret and their pets from the 1940s, or the more variegated versions of modern royal souvenirs), then Jacobite kitsch can be seen as a projection of Scottish national identity, suitably distanced from enduring relevance. Jacobitism's association with political immaturity in the fiction of Scott and Whig historiography's account of an independent Scotland can thus be seen as reflected in the iconography of a boyish and sanitised Charles Edward, not a king but best a prince, and too young to govern. (It has, after all, taken Scottish historiography almost 300 years to return to the position of seeing Scotland as '"different" rather than backward' (Kidd, 1994, 12). The '45 becomes a wild adolescent adventure, of the sort which tempted the romantic in Edward Waverley. Jacobitism is thus aligned with all the historiographical constructions of Scotland's immaturity as a country which so beset the eighteenth century, and which have been discussed in the earlier sections of this study. At the same time, it provides a comforting surrogate national identity, as Scott did in his 1822 pageant: just as tartan synecdochally stands for Scotland, so does the Jacobitism with which it is associated. This comforting surrogacy is, however, undermined by the flavour of immaturity, irrelevance and defeat which surrounds Jacobitism, although it is on the contrary conditionally reinforced through its adoption by the British establishment. Queen Victoria's strong links with tartanry in the decoration of Balmoral and elsewhere are of twofold interest here. In the first place, her use of tartan helped to consolidate a role of military leadership or at least participation, a difficult role for a woman in earlier centuries to secure; in the second, it conflated her identity with Jacobite identity. As the Queen herself said, 'for Stuart blood is in my veins and I am now, their representative and the people are as devoted and loyal to me, as they were to that unhappy Race' (of course, they were not particularly loyal, or the Stuarts would still be with us; but such a construction rendered the loss more poignant, and made the successful Hanoverian absorption of its iconography more absolute). The heritage portrayal of the Scottish nation was part of the heritage of the British state, and thus indissolubly linked to it. No doubt Queen Victoria's final rehabilitation of the Jacobite song (begun forty years earlier) and the Prince Consort's posing as a heroic hunter of a bygone age were parts of the same construction of incorporation which celebrated a jacobitical Scottish national identity while rendering it part of a broader British heritage. It is thus paradoxically the simultaneously mocked and valorised role of Jacobitism which provides the basis for the 'assurance' of a history which bypasses it even while yielding its accessories the centre stage.[7]

In this context, it is small wonder that many twentieth-century Scottish patriots have scorned the relevance of Jacobitism to Scotland (though, as I have argued elsewhere, this ignores the continuing relevance of the radical Jacobite critique, still acknowledged in unlikely quarters: as for example the 1994 Scottish Republican discussion document, *Jacobites or Covenanters: Which Tradition?*). Nevertheless, we may do right if we feel uneasy about the degree of demythologisation which has challenged the kitsch of tartanry in the last quarter of a century. As argued in the Introduction, in the case of the Myth of the Jacobite Clans, such demythologisation is effectively only the creation of a new myth. In Scottish popular history and cultural studies, the exposure of so-called 'myths' to which our cultural identity has been in thrall has become quite an industry. This exposure of 'myths' is held to be of service. I cannot find it so, nor think it a coincidence that one of the strongest proponents among British historians of the benefits of Union, Lord Dacre, has written one of the most influential essays on the subject (in *The Invention of Tradition*). For, as in the case of the Myth of the Jacobite Clans, the destruction of myths is itself a manifestation of the values of a centring 'British' history. The attack on tartanry is only a further attack on self, yet another example of those earlier attacks which themselves were responsible for simultaneously limiting and exaggerating the role of tartan in Scottish identity. The self-belief evident in the sculpture of the Children of Lir in Dublin is very different from the material manifestations of kitsch in Scotland; but this is not the problem of myths but the problem of what is done with them. The fragmentary, detached and exaggerated qualities of the Scottish past are the result of a previous defeat by a historical rhetoric which now revisits them in order to berate them for what it has made them. Jacobitism is historically significant as an expression of Scottish national identity, a major military threat to the British state, and an ingenious, varied and socially diverse set of cultural images and values. The aestheticised representations through which it has been controlled and turned to kitsch are not the phenomenon itself, but the counterparts of the demythologisers who mock them. The reification of Jacobite romance is not the reality of Jacobite purpose. In this context, those who seek a critique of the shortbread tones of Tory kitsch through a more 'patriotic' stripping-away of the tartan cult succeed sometimes only in an equality of misrepresentation. The 'Highland Cult' is too complicated a phenomenon to be amenable to deconstruction – for its destroyer stands on the historical ground it has long claimed as its own. The military prowess of Scotland abroad and the provincial character of Scotland at home are both tightly thirled to the Myth of the Jacobite Clans: a story of an isolated provincial society which made its mark on the world only through loyalty, true or misplaced, and a glamorous violence now reduced to commodity or the tokenistic qualities of identity manifest in the campaign to keep the Scottish battalions.[8]

The myth is, nevertheless, one of the chief ways in which Jacobite imagery and products are linked to British identity. Not only are there the tartan-military and national-cultural dimensions of commercial Jacobite iconography; there is also the importance of commodity as an expression of the diversity of empire and its inheritance, an importance rooted in nineteenth-century England, but which still informs the productions of Scottish kitsch: 'the Great Exhibition of 1851 had at its root a single conception: that all human life and endeavour could be fully represented by exhibiting manufactured articles' (Richards, 1990, 17). The importance of commodities as the expression of historicity was developed through the 'bricolage' of the Great Exhibition to the full status of kitsch by the Golden Jubilee of 1887, when royal, national, religious and sentimental icons were rendered more intensely material than ever before. The contemporaneity of this with the cult of the Celt, evident throughout the 1880s and 1890s, helped to emplace jacobitical representations of Scotland ever more firmly in the zone of commodity. This was no doubt abetted by the 'revival of a very old idea, that the reigning monarch had two bodies' in the iconography of the Jubilee period (Richards, 95). The intensity of late Victorian kitsch no doubt also succoured the nostalgic constructs of Lowland Presbyterian Scotland being put together by the Kailyard group of writers, as well as (in the Diamond Jubilee in particular) emphasising the military aspect of 'the phantasmagoria of Empire'. This was what the *Daily Mail*, 'in headlines of gold ink on June 21, 1897, called the "GREATNESS OF THE BRITISH RACE"' (Richards, 95, 116). 'Conservative pride in local colour and traditions went well with the grand design' of such imperial celebration, and tartan must have received a renewed boost from the military connotations of the 'heroic and romantic vision of Empire' celebrated in British popular art at the end of the nineteenth century. At the same time, tartanry's use had already anticipated the themes of 'domestication and reconciliation . . . persistent elements in her [Britain's] exhibitions from 1851'.[9]

The developing heroicisation of Empire can be seen in the intensely patriotic reaction to Scottish troops in military engagements in the later nineteenth century. That weathervane of the commonplace, William McGonagall, proudly described their achievements, as did others such as A. C. MacDonell, who in *Lays of the Heather* (1896), a collection remarkably dedicated to 'H.R.H. Prince Rupert of Bavaria, Heir of the Royal House of Stuart' (as he indeed was), celebrated the transposition of Scottish localities to imperial destiny, a celebration rendered in predominantly Highland terms. In 'Lochaber's Sons', the locality of the 'depths of far Lochaber' is transposed to the arena of international militarism, which nevertheless keeps its domestic dimension: 'E'en the tartan that they wore / Bore witness to the ties of yore'. In 'The Seaforth Highlanders of Hindoostan', the tartan is an insignia of bravery, reliability and imperial provincial identity submerged in greater British purpose:

> O'er the giddy heights of Savendroog the kilt and sporran
> swung,
> The first to dare the steep descent by jagged peaks o'erhung;
> The first the dread ascent to gain, three hundred feet *en face*,
> Climbing the perilous rock by dint of tufts of slippery grass.
> Then burst the belching batteries forth, where shot and shell
> betrayed
> Within the fort the dusky hordes, by British pluck dismayed.
> 'Britons strike home!'

The provincial skill of the Highlanders as mountaineers here serves the imperial purpose, sublimated as it is into pan-imperial language as 'British pluck'. Their badge of locality's worth and dignity resides in its role as the mark of imperial loyalty and success, while the presence of Highland troops in places with such remote and exotic names reassuringly reconciles their role with British aims while alienising someone else. The Highlanders are now 'Britons', their qualities including English public-school 'pluck' as well as native mountaineering talent; this new identity is reinforced in the objectification of its opponent, 'the dusky hordes' of dark dehumanised orientals. Yet if the 'kilt and sporran' still 'swung' for a Jacobite leader rather than Kipling's 'Widow o' Windsor', it would be the Highlanders who would be the cannibals or 'hordes', unclean, verminous and un-British, as their grandfathers had been.[10] If jacobitised tartanry is so crucially linked to military loyalty and local colour in its traditional use, it is hardly surprising that the decline of imperial power and participation has led to a recrudescence of distrust in such symbols. The 'imperial resonance' of Balmorality and its trappings are manifestations of a political world which has been diminishing in reality for some time. It is perhaps only because, as Enoch Powell said in 1946, that 'the life of nations no less than that of men is lived largely in the imagination', that the links between Scotland and its past and Scotland and Britain forged by kitsch to the world are enduring ones. That the realm of such endurance is narrowing a little is perhaps visible in the claim for Britain of a supreme cultural heritage, rather than any other kind of achievement. Where once the cultural iconography of royal, national and military kitsch was merely representational of a broader ascendancy, it now appears more and more an end in itself, an series of icons which are their own idols. This heritage increasingly indicates the authority and autonomy of the British past without importing such status into the present: hence the visible social nostalgia of particularly (though not only) Conservative politicians. In Scotland, where the jacobitised past has in a special sense been marginal for much longer, its status seems less and less central: hence the many exercises in demythologisation of the last twenty years. However, as I have argued, the truth about the character of Jacobitism itself is much more important to a full historical understanding of the Scottish story which we inherit than the demythologisers often allow; in any case, their verdict is often uncomfortably close to that practised by old-fashioned Whig historiography. That that verdict is inadequate, I trust has been shown; though it is an understandable conclusion to have reached in the project of disassembling Scottish provincial imperial identity in order to uncover a 'genuine' underlying national identity. So deep is the imperial concept of British partnership still ingrained in Scotland in the post-imperial age, however, that the newly-discovered 'genuine' identity is arguably more of a reaction than an evaluation. Over-emphasis on the radical or egalitarian qualities of Scottish cultural and intellectual life, the 'democratic intellect', corporatism, social concern, and the cultural autonomy of post-Union Scotland, are signs of a trend which surely grievously underestimates the power and centrality of Scotland's role as coloniser, not colonised, or even (as sometimes seems implied) entirely absent in spirit from the British Empire. The inferiorism found in the narratives of Scotland's past is the counterpart of its romanticisation; but the answer is not to deromanticise but to understand *why* romanticisation took place, and to understand also the underlying danger of the historical challenge which led to the incorporation and distancing characteristic of romance's politically neutralising style.[11]

And yet still the lustre of depoliticised sentiment casts a glow over political defeat symbolised by images torn out of history to grace the niches of romantic veneration and its commercial pastiche. They are thrust out from the contextualising world of fact, the struggle to be Scotland rather than remember it. So between Holyrood and the Castle, Charles Edward smiles from a thousand whisky bottles and shortbread tins, trailing like a cloud the glorious myth of his selfless and romantic Highland clans in the heart of the Lowland commerce which supposedly rejected them, while the times in which he lived and the political and ideological context of those who supported his cause are alike lost in the traffic of popular culture which celebrates the myth, and the high culture which judges and scorns it. The Myth of the Jacobite Clans is the closest that Kailyard comes to history. As Scotland's heritage, it is protected by cultural and commercial authorities, native and expatriate, who inherit the bifurcated role of Jacobite tartanry, romantic and irrelevant. This book has endeavoured to show what this heritage is, where it comes from, and what relation it bears to the Rising of 1745, as its sales and images roll over another anniversary.

Notes

Introduction

1. Herbert Butterfield, *The Whig Interpretation of History* (London: G. Bell & Sons, 1931), 3, 16; E. H. Dance, in Otto-Ernst Schuddehopf et al. (eds), *History Teaching and History Textbook Revision* (Strasbourg: Centre for Cultural Co-operation of the Council of Europe, 1967), 77, 85; Max Weber, *Essays on Sociology*, cited in Peter Heeks, 'Myth, History and Theory', *History and Theory* 33:1 (1994), 15; Gilles Deleuze, cited in Sande Cohen, *Historical Culture: On the Recording of an Academic Discipline* (Berkeley, Los Angeles and London: University of California Press, 1986), x.

2. Work has carried on concerning the numbers and origin of Jacobite recruits in 1745 since the late nineteenth century – in Rosebery's *List of Persons Concerned in the Rebellion*, in the work of Sir Bruce Seton and Jean McCann, on the muster rolls since 1914, and in particular geographical areas (especially north-east Scotland). These findings have perhaps not been adequately collated or measured against each other: in addition, there is considerable unpublished material in the Scottish intelligence reports as well as useful additional details in the reports of the Commissioners of Excise and elsewhere. These are all brought together in this study to give an in-depth assessment of the location and strength of Scottish Jacobite forces in 1745: moreover, some fresh comparative details are offered on the Rising of 1715, which has been even more incompletely analysed. The comparison of figures from both risings with those uncovered by scholars in the Covenanting period is instructive.

3. This line comes from the National Trust for Scotland slideshow at Culloden Battlefield Centre, which attracts around 125,000 visitors each year.
4. For the enduring German accent of the Hanoverian family, see Tom Nairn, *The Enchanted Glass* (London: Radius, 1988), 68.
5. Heeks (1994), 1, 2.
6. James Young, 'Forging the Nation', *Cencrastus* 49 (1994), 40–1.
7. Cf. the discussion in Murray G. H. Pittock, *The Invention of Scotland* (London and New York: Routledge, 1991), 138.
8. Cf. my article, 'Forging North Britain in the Age of Macpherson', in *The Edinburgh Review* (Spring 1995), forthcoming.
9. Cf. Colin Kidd, *Scotlands* 1 (1994), 1–17.
10. The clan graves and monument at Culloden are themselves mementoes of the romantic jacobitisation of Scotland in the nineteenth century, being associated with the largely sentimental *fin-de-siècle* cult of the Stuarts: cf. Murray G. H. Pittock, 'Decadence and the English Tradition', unpublished D.Phil. thesis (Oxford University, 1986).
11. Cf. Pittock (1991), ch. 3.
12. Frank McLynn, *Charles Edward Stuart* (London: Routledge, 1988), 202 for total strength of the second army; National Library of Scotland MS 17514, f. 119 indicates Jacobite estimates of their own strength. In this context, it seems that modern historians are themselves victims of the fluid boundary of identity between 'Highlander' and 'Scot', which, developing in the icons and ideology of Jacobitism itself, was adopted in an inflated and commercial way in the nineteenth century. Thus perhaps does cultural inheritance dictate historiographical choice.
13. Frank McLynn, *The Jacobite Army in England: The Final Campaign* (Edinburgh: John Donald, 1983), 79 for the quotation from the eminent Whig.
14. Cf. John Robertson, *The Scottish Enlightenment and the Militia Issue* (Edinburgh: John Donald, 1985), 99; G. M. Trevelyan, *England under the Stuarts*, Volume 5 of *A History of England* in 8 volumes, gen. ed. Sir Charles Oman KBE, 19th edn (London: Methuen, 1947), 378, 379; Trevelyan, *History of England*, 3rd edn (London, New York and Toronto: Longmans, Green & Co., 1952), 536, 538; Charles Chevenix Trench, *George II* (London: Allen Lane, 1973), 234, 236; Justin McCarthy, *A History of the Four Georges*, 4 vols (London: Chatto & Windus, 1890), vol. 2, p. 276; Bruce Lenman, *The Jacobite Clans of the Great Glen* (London: Methuen, 1984); John, Master of Sinclair, *Memoirs of the Insurrection in Scotland in 1715*, ed. messrs

MacKnight and Lang, with notes by Sir Walter Scott, Bart (Edinburgh: Abbotsford Club, 1858), xi, 86.

15. Basil Williams, *The Whig Supremacy 1714–1760* (Oxford: Clarendon Press, 1952 (1939)), 243; J. R. Green, *A Short History of the English People* (London: Macmillan and Co., 1875), 724; *Cassell's History of the British People V: From the Revolutionary Settlement to Waterloo* (London: The Waverley Book Co., 1923), 1630, 1633; Samuel R. Gardiner DCL LLD, *A Student's History of England from the Earliest Times to the Death of King Edward VII*, new edn (London, New York, Bombay and Calcutta: Longmans, Green & Co., 1910), 740; A. V. Dicey and Robert S. Rait, *Thoughts on the Union Between England and Scotland* (London: Macmillan, 1920), 305; A. D. Innes, *A History of the British Nation From the Earliest Times to the Present Day* (London and Edinburgh: T. C. & E. C. Jack, 1912), 601; Sir Winston S. Churchill, *A History of the English-Speaking Peoples*, 7 vols (London: Cassell and Company Ltd, 1957), vol. 3, p. 109; James Michael Hill, *Celtic Warfare 1595–1763* (Edinburgh: John Donald, 1986), 1, 106; Robert M. Rayner, *A Concise History of Britain* (London, New York and Toronto: Longmans, Green & Co., 1941), 386–7; McCarthy (1890), 294; Keith Feiling, *A History of England From the Coming of the English to 1918* (London: Macmillan, 1950), 663; Charles Macfarlane and Thomas Thomson, *The Comprehensive History of England*, 4 vols (Oxford, Glasgow, Edinburgh and London: Blackie & Son, 1861), vol. 3, pp. 275, 284, 289 (Macfarlane and Thomson's characterisation of the Highland army as partly non-Highland seems rather uncertain); Sir Fitzroy Maclean, *A Concise History of Scotland* (London: Thames & Hudson, 1988 (1970)), 171, 174; Sir George Clark, *English History: A Survey* (Oxford: Clarendon Press, 1971). For the conventional organisation of the Jacobite army, see National Library of Scotland MS 3787 (Order Book of Appin's Regiment) and *The Miscellany of the Spalding Club*, vol. 1 (Aberdeen, 1841), 275–345 (Day Book of Ogilvy's (Forfarshire) Regiment); also Bruce Lenman, *The Jacobite Cause* (Glasgow: Richard Drew and National Trust for Scotland, 1986), 106. Stephen Wood, *The Auld Alliance* (Edinburgh: Mainstream, 1989), 77–86 deals with the military careers of exiled Jacobites, as does Frank McLynn, *The Jacobites* (London: Routledge, 1985), 130ff.; cf. Mary Beacock Fryer, *Allan Maclean: Jacobite General* (Toronto: Dundurn Press, 1987). See also Sir Bruce Seton of Ancrum, Bart, and Jean Gordon Arnot, *The Prisoners of the '45*, Scottish History Society, 3 vols (Edinburgh: Edinburgh University Press, 1928/9), vol. 3, pp. 308–9 for Sharp.

16. Paul Langford, *A Polite and Commercial People* (Oxford: Clarendon

Press, 1989), 197; Linda Colley, *Britons* (Yale: Yale University Press, 1992), 81 and passim; R. H. Campbell, *Scotland Since 1707*, 2nd edn (Edinburgh: John Donald, 1985 (1965)), 7; Annette Smith, 'Dundee and the '45', in Lesley Scott-Moncrieff (ed.), *The '45: To Gather an Image Whole* (Edinburgh: The Mercat Press, 1988), 108; J. G. A. Pocock, 'The Limits and Divisions of British History: In Search of an Unknown Subject', *American Historical Review* 87 (1982), 328 (see also idem, 'British History: A Plea for a New Subject', *Journal of Modern History* 47:4 (1975), 601–21, 626–8 for the start of the debate); Geoffrey Holmes and Daniel Szechi, *The Age of Oligarchy* (London: Longmans, 1993); Alistair and Henrietta Tayler, *Jacobites of Aberdeenshire and Banffshire in the Rising of 1715* (Edinburgh and London: Oliver & Boyd, 1934), vii.

17. E. H. Carr, *What is History?*, 2nd edn (London: Penguin, 1990 (1987)), 12, 23.

18. John Prebble, *The King's Jaunt* (London, 1988) for Scott's contribution; William Ferguson, *Scotland 1689 to the Present* (Edinburgh: Oliver and Boyd, 1968), 149–50; Frank McLynn (1985), 80.

19. James MacKnight, in Sinclair (1858), xxiii.

20. G. R. Elton, *Political History: Principle and Practice* (Allen Lane: Penguin Press, 1970), 4; Butterfield (1931), 64; Hayden White, cited in Lionel Gossman, 'Towards a Rational Historiography', *Transactions of the American Philosophical Society*, 79:3 (1989), 28.

21. Rosalind Mitchison, 'Patriotism and National Identity in Eighteenth-century Scotland', in T. W. Moody (ed.), *Nationality and the Pursuit of National Independence* (Belfast: The Appletree Press, 1978), 94ff.

Chapter 1

1. Hugh A. MacDougall, *Racial Myth in English History* (Montreal: Harvest House; Hanover, NH and London: University Press of New England, 1982), 3, 77; Colin Kidd, *Subverting Scotland's Past*, Cambridge: Cambridge University Press, 1993), 125; W. Blaikie Murdoch, cited in Pittock (1991), 124; Pittendrigh Macgillavray, ibid. (address to the '45 Club, 1911): 127.

2. Jeremy Black, *Culloden and the '45* (Stroud: Alan Sutton, 1990); Gerald Newman, *The Rise of English Nationalism* (London: Weidenfeld & Nicolson, 1987), 54ff., 75, 123; cf. Ernest Gellner, *Nations and Nationalism* (Oxford: Basil Blackwell, 1983), 63, 138, and idem, *Plough, Sword and Book: The Structure of Human History* (London and Glasgow: Paladin, 1991 (1988)), 36, 61; cf. the argument in Pittock (1991).

3. Colley (1992), 1, 6, 11; Newman (1987), 75, 123; cf. Pittock, address to the Royal Society of Edinburgh (BP Prize Lecture), 25 October 1993.

4. Stanley Baldwin, *On England* (1926), quoted in John Osmond, *The Divided Kingdom*, A Channel Four Book (London: Constable, 1988), 157; John Major's April 1993 Mansion House speech, *The Independent*, 5 August 1993, 4.

5. Cf. Murray G. H. Pittock, *Poetry and Jacobite Politics in Eighteenth-Century Britain and Ireland* (Cambridge: Cambridge University Press, 1994), especially chs 2 and 4 for this discussion in more detail; Michael Lynch, *Scotland: A New History* (London: Century, 1991), 344 for Bute cartoon; John Ashton, *Chap-Books of the Eighteenth Century* (London: Chatto & Windus, 1882), 476.

6. Ashton (1882), ibid.

7. G. M. Trevelyan, *England Under the Stuarts* (London: Methuen, 1947 (1904)), 402; Kidd (1993), passim; F. W. Robertson, *The Scottish Way 1746–1946* (Rothesay, 1946), 3; Michael Turnbull (ed.), *The Poems of John Davidson*, 2 vols (Edinburgh: Scottish Academic Press, 1973), vol. 1, p. 226.

8. Kidd (1993), 248; Peter Womack, *Improvement and Romance* (Basingstoke: Macmillan, 1989), 1; see Pittock (1991), ch. 4.

9. Lynch (1991), 299; cf. Pittock (1994), ch. 1 for a discussion of Philp's *Grameid*; NLS MS 9202; James Hogg, *The Jacobite Relics*, 2 vols (Edinburgh, 1819/21), vol. 2, pp. 78, 115; Norval Clyne, *The Scottish Jacobites and their Poetry* (Aberdeen, 1887), 29; *Letters of John Graham of Claverhouse, Viscount of Dundee with Illustrative Documents*, ed. George Smythe, Bannatyne Club (Edinburgh: James Ballatyne & Co., 1826), 47.

10. Cf. my article on 'Jacobite Culture', forthcoming in 'Charlie's Year' (HMSO; Glasgow Museums, 1995).

11. Cf. Pittock (1994), passim.

12. Cf. I. S. Robinson, 'Pope Gregory VII, the Princes and the Pactum 1077–1080', *English Historical Review* 94 (1979), 721–56; cf. John Miller, 'Catholic Officers in the Later Stuart Army', *English Historical Review* 88 (1973), 35–53; also John Childs, *The Army, James II and the Glorious Revolution* (Manchester: Manchester University Press, 1980); Robin D. Gwynn, 'James II in the Light of his Treatment of the Huguenot Refugees in England, 1685–1686', *English Historical Review* 92 (1977), 820–33; MacDougall (1982), 43, 49, 103, Acton cited, 110; Susan Maclean Kybett, *Bonnie Prince Charlie* (London, 1988); Trevelyan (1952), 356, 365; The Rt Hon. The Earl of Birkenhead, *Turning Points in History* (London:

Hutchinson & Co., n.d), 107, 112 for a traditionally negative portrait of James VII and II.

13. Bruce Lenman, 'The Scottish Nobility and the Revolution of 1688–90', in Robert Beddard (ed.), *The Revolutions of 1688* (Oxford: Clarendon Press, 1991), 161; *The Collected Essays of Christopher Hill Volume 1: Writing and Revolution in 17th Century England* (Brighton: The Harvester Press, 1985), 115; P. Hume Brown, *The Legislative Union of England and Scotland* (Oxford: Clarendon Press, 1914), 58.

14. Alexander Carlyle, cited in John Robertson, *The Scottish Enlightenment and the Militia Issue* (Edinburgh: John Donald, 1985), 99.

15. Marinell Ash, *The Strange Death of Scottish History* (Edinburgh: Ramsay Head Press, 1980), 22, 23, for Kames and Tytler, 34 for debate over the antiquarian society; idem, 'William Wallace and Robert the Bruce: The Life and Death of a National Myth', in Raphael Samuel and Paul Thompson (eds), *The Myths We Live By* (London and New York: Routledge, 1990), 90; Lynch (1991), 343; Michael Fry, 'The Whig Interpretation of Scottish History', in Ian Donnachie and Christopher Whatley (eds), *The Manufacture of Scottish History* (Edinburgh: Polygon, 1992), 83; *The Edinburgh Review*, cited in Nicholas Phillipson, *Hume* (London: Weidenfeld & Nicolson, 1989), 32; Kidd (1993), 210; for the 'old' and 'new' in Scott, see Murray G. H. Pittock, 'Scott as Historiographer: The Case of *Waverley*', in D. S. Hewitt and J. H. Alexander (eds), *Scott in Carnival* (Aberdeen: Association for Scottish Literary Studies, 1993), 145–53.

16. Kidd (1993), 267, 280.

17. Ibid., 29, 214, 267, 279, 280.

18. Murray G. H. Pittock, *Clio's Clavers* (Edinburgh: Leerie Books, 1992), 10; Kidd (1993), 213; Womack (1989), 85.

19. Kidd (1993), 223 for Macpherson's Whiggery; Fiona Stafford, *The Sublime Savage* (Edinburgh: Edinburgh University Press, 1988), 18, 20; George Pratt Insh, *The Scottish Jacobite Movement* (Edinburgh and London, 1952), 174.

20. Cf. Pittock (1991), ch. 3; idem (1994), ch. 4.

21. Clare O'Halloran, 'Irish Re-creations of the Gaelic Past: The Challenge of Macpherson's Ossian', *Past and Present* 124 (1989), 72; Kidd (1993), 253 for a discussion of Pinkerton.

22. Hugh Trevor-Roper, 'The Invention of Tradition: The Highland Tradition of Scotland', in Eric Hobsbawm and Terence Ranger (eds), *The Invention of Tradition* (Cambridge: Cambridge University Press,

1983), 15; Colley (1992), 86; Kidd (1993), 233ff.; Pittock (1991), 73, 78 and passim.
23. Stafford (1988), 178, 182; Womack (1989), 26; Sir George Mackenzie, *A Defence of the Antiquity of the Royal Line of Scotland* (London: printed for R. C., 1685), 83.
24. Cf. Pittock (1991, 1994); also 'Sources and Dates for the Jacobite Song', *Archives* (1993), 25–9.
25. Hill (1986); Bruce Lenman, *Integration, Enlightenment and Industrialization* (London: Edward Arnold, 1981), 65–6.

Chapter 2

1. Bruce Lenman, *The Jacobite Risings in Britain 1689–1746* (London: Methuen, 1980), 87; Jean McCann, 'The Organisation of the Jacobite Army in 1745–46', unpublished Ph.D. thesis (University of Edinburgh, 1963), 108; Christopher Harvie, *Scotland and Nationalism*, 2nd edn (London and New York: Routledge, 1994), 44.
2. *Letters of Viscount Dundee* (1826), 42; *Memoirs of Sir Ewen Cameron of Lochiell*, ed. Bindon Blood and James MacKnight (Edinburgh: Abbotsford Club, 1842), 251.
3. *Lochiell* (1842), 369n and passim; Magnus Linklater and Christian Hesketh, *For King and Conscience: John Graham of Claverhouse, Viscount Dundee (1648–1689)* (London: Weidenfeld & Nicolson, 1989), 171, 179, 200, 222, 224.
4. Cf. Edward M. Furgol, *A Regimental History of the Covenanting Armies, 1639–1651* (Edinburgh: John Donald, 1990); David Stevenson, *Revolution and Counter-Revolution in Scotland 1644–1657* (London: Royal Historical Society, 1977) does not significantly disagree with Furgol's figures.
5. Michael Lynch (1991), 319.
6. For a discussion of the 'conservative north', see Gordon Donaldson, *Scottish Church History* (Edinburgh: Scottish Academic Press, 1985); David Stevenson, *The Scottish Revolution, 1637–1644* (Newton Abbot: David & Charles, 1973), 71, 92, 139, 146; Daniel Szechi, *Jacobitism and Tory Politics 1710–14* (Edinburgh: John Donald, 1984), 63–4; Szechi (ed.), *Letters of George Lockhart of Carnwath*, Scottish History Society 5:2 (Edinburgh: Scottish History Society, 1989), 53n, 57n, 58n, 75n, 76n, 85n, 93n and passim.
7. Duncan Fraser, *Montrose (before 1700)* (Montrose: Standard Press, 1970), 85–6, 90; Gordon Donaldson (1985), 191, 200.
8. McCann (1963), 137, 146, 147; Rev. Canon George Farquhar, *The*

Episcopal History of Perth (Perth: James H. Jackson, 1894), 171; Gibson (1988), 9; Fraser (1970), 169; Alexander Keith, *A Thousand Years of Aberdeen* (Aberdeen: Aberdeen University Press, 1972), 134–5; Peter F. Anson, *Underground Catholicism in Scotland 1622–1878* (Montrose: Standard Press, 1970), 102, 111, 113 and passim; W. B. Blaikie (1916), 127. Cf. also G. D. Henderson, *Mystics of the North East* (Aberdeen: Third Spalding Club, 1934).

9. Lynch (1991), 328; Alistair and Henrietta Tayler, *1715: The Story of the Rising* (London and Edinburgh: Thomas Nelson, 1936), 31, 52, 338 and passim.

10. Taylers (1936), 39 and passim; Patten's list is reproduced in Christopher Sinclair-Stevenson, *Inglorious Rebellion* (London: Hamish Hamilton, 1971), 195–8.

11. John Baynes, *The Jacobite Rising of 1715* (London: Cassell, 1970), 59, 71, 225n for Rae's figures; Taylers (1936), 72, 95; NLS MS 1498; cf. Sinclair-Stevenson (1971), 97n, 113.

12. National Library of Scotland MS 874 ('Information of A. B. to J. C. . . .') for Mar's 46 battalions; NLS MS 1498 for 'List of the King's Army' on 5 November 1715; Baynes (1970), 75, 98, 131, 133; Sinclair (1858), 73.

13. Keith (1972), 273; Hogg (1819/21), vol. 2, p. 43 for 'The Piper of Dundee'; James Thomson, *The History of Dundee* (Dundee: John Durkan & Son, 1874), 112–14; Elizabeth Carmichael, 'Jacobitism in the Scottish Commission of the Peace, 1707–1760', *Scottish Historical Review* 58 (1979), 58–69; Argyll to Townshend, quoted in Taylers (1936), 60; Banff lairds and reports to Lord Justice Clerk, 173, 176.

14. Lockhart (1989), 161; Lynch (1991), 320 for malt-tax riots.

15. *List of Persons Concerned in the Rebellion*, with a Preface by the Earl of Rosebery and Annotations by the Rev. Walter MacLeod, Publications of the Scottish History Society, vol. 8 (Edinburgh: Edinburgh University Press, 1890), x, xv, xvi.

16. For a discussion of the Highlander as patriot, see Pittock (1991, 1994); for Charles Edward and Republican imagery, cf. Paul Monod, *Jacobitism and the English People* (Cambridge: Cambridge University Press, 1989).

17. 'The Highlanders at Macclesfield in 1745', *Scottish Historical Review* 5 (1908), 288; McLynn, *Jacobite Army* (1983), 28; Lenman (1986), 105; Sir Bruce Seton, Bart, 'Dress of the Jacobite Army', *Scottish Historical Review* 25 (1928), 273, 274, 277, 278, 279; Leah Leneman, *Living in Atholl 1685–1785* (Edinburgh: Edinburgh University Press, 1986), 168ff. for lack of tangible distinction in estate records between Highlanders and Lowlanders; William Donaldson, *The Jacobite Song*

(Aberdeen: Aberdeen University Press, 1988) for Episcopal and Catholic attitudes towards Gaelic.

18. McLynn, *Jacobite Army* (1983), 24–5, 31 for number of camp-followers; R. Murdoch-Lawrence, 'Aberdeen Women as Jacobites', *Aberdeen Journal: Notes and Queries* 1 (1908), 49; Rosebery (1890), xvi, xvii; McCann (1963), xi; Geoffrey Holmes and Daniel Szechi, *The Age of Oligarchy: Pre-industrial Britain 1722–1783* (London and New York: Longman, 1993), 99; Daniel Szechi and David Hayton, 'John Bull's Other Kingdoms: The English Government of Scotland and Ireland', in Clyve Jones (ed.), *Britain in the First Age of Party 1680–1750* (London and Ronceverte: Hambledon Press, 1987), 256; Lord Elcho, *A Short Account of the Affairs of Scotland*, ed. Hon. Evan Charteris (Edinburgh: David Douglas, 1907), 424–5 for size of Cumberland's army (Cumberland Papers quoted 425n); Hilary Kemp, *The Jacobite Rebellion* (London: Almark Publishing, 1975).

19. See Kidd (1994) for the debate over the famine figures; Lynch (1991), 280; Michael Flinn et al. (eds), *Scottish Population History from the 17th Century to the 1930s* (Cambridge: Cambridge University Press, 1977), 8, 144ff., 180, 198–9, 200; Furgol (1990), 4–6. Paul Hopkins, in *Glencoe and the End of the Highland War* (Edinburgh: John Donald, 1986), reminds us (314) of the very small size of the Scottish army in the 1680s.

20. Stevenson (1973) for the royalist figures (e.g. p. 146); NLS MS 17523, f. 196 for the situation in Orkney at 23 June 1746; NLS MS 17522, ff. 109–10, 111–15, 117–30 also concern Jacobite activity there.

21. McCann (1963), xi–xvi, 5 (it is noteworthy, however, that only 2562 from the clans are listed with Mar on 5 November in NLS MS 1498); McLynn, *Jacobite Army* (1983), 27 roughly tallies; Seton and Arnot (1928/9), vol. 1. For Kemp, see n. 18 above.

22. Alastair Livingstone of Bachuil et al. (eds), *Muster Roll of Prince Charles Edward Stuart's Army 1745–46*, with an introduction by Bruce Lenman (Aberdeen: Aberdeen University Press, 1984), passim; NLS MS 290 gives Blaikie's list of Jacobite officers in 1745 by location. References to Webster are to James Gray Kidd (ed.), *Scottish Population Statistics*, Publications of the Scottish History Society, 3rd Series, vol. 44 (Edinburgh: T. & A. Constable, 1952).

23. Thomson (1874), 118. Thomson makes some hardly significant exceptions to this statement. Smith (1988), 107.

24. *Jacobite Correspondence of The Atholl Family During the Rebellion, 1745–46*, ed. messrs Burton and Laing (Edinburgh: Abbotsford Club, 1840), 96ff. for details of the carts and transport for the cargo; cf. also McCann (1963), 102; NLS MS 17514, f. 56 for arming of Jacobite forces;

ff. 87, 97, 109, 119–26 for intelligence reports on Jacobite forces at this time; f. 129 for General Blakeney's intelligence; *The Miscellany of the Spalding Club*, vol. 1 (1841), 347–98 (Rev. Bisset's account – particularly 352, 356) for Jacobite recruiting and activity in Aberdeen; Alistair and Henrietta Tayler, *Jacobites of Aberdeenshire and Banffshire in the Forty-Five* (Aberdeen: Milne & Hutchison, 1928), 228.

25. For East Lothian Jacobitism, see W. Forbes Gray and James H. Jamieson, *A Short History of Haddington* (Edinburgh: Neill & Co., 1944), 56; NLS MS 17525, f. 139ff. for reports on the guard in Edinburgh; MS 2960 for the list of ladies; Bishop Robert Forbes, *The Lyon in Mourning*, ed. Henry Paton, Scottish History Society, 3 vols (Edinburgh: Edinburgh University Press, 1895), vol. 2, pp. 221–2 for trouble in Edinburgh in 1748; ibid., vol. 3, p. 305ff. for Episcopalian congregations in 1770s; McLynn (1988), 148.

26. Taylers (1928), 8, 357; *Memoirs of the Rebellion in Aberdeen and Banff*, in Walter Biggar Blaikie (ed.), *Origins of the 'Forty-Five: And Other Papers Relating to that Rising* (Edinburgh: T. & A. Constable, 1916), 135ff., 163n; NLS MS 3142, f. 84 for city being 'overaw'd'; for report on sentiments of Loudon's militia and other relevant details, see Rev. Bisset's narrative in *The Miscellany of the Spalding Club* (1841); Sir Robert Gordon of Gordonstown to Alexander Brodie, Lord Lyon, quoted in Alistair and Henrietta Tayler, *Jacobites of Aberdeenshire and Banffshire in the Rising of 1715* (Edinburgh and London: Oliver and Boyd, 1934), vii on the vitality of north-east Jacobitism.

27. Farquhar (1894), 165 for Charles Edward's visit to St John's; Lenman (1980), 257 for Jacobite difficulties in 1745; NLS MS 17514, ff. 108, 244.

28. *Atholl Correspondence* (1840), 16; NLS MS 17514, f. 190 for the efforts of Wallace and Erskine; J. M. McBain, *Arbroath: Past and Present* (Arbroath: Brodie & Salmond, 1887), 342.

29. Cf. Taylers (1928), 8; Blaikie (1916), 124; *The Miscellany of the Spalding Club*, vols 1 (1841) and 4 (1849), 321–2; NLS Advocates MS 23.3.28 (Eaglescarnie Papers), ff. 96, 277.

30. NLS MS 17514, f. 271 for the situation in Badenoch and Aberdeenshire; f. 274 for attitude of the disaffected; f. 275 for the Dingwall incident; NLS MS 17505 for Kirriemuir patrol; Taylers (1928), passim, and Alexander Mackintosh, *The Muster Roll of the Forfarshire or Lord Ogilvy's Regiment* (Inverness: The Northern Counties Newspaper & Printing & Publishing Co., 1914), x for post-1745 trouble.

31. National Library of Scotland MS 3142, f. 49 for numbers defending Edinburgh in 1745; Furgol (1990), 42, 133 for Covenanting force

raised in Edinburgh; NLS MS 290 for number of officers from Edinburgh; for the population of UK cities and the proportion in various occupations in the eighteenth century, see Holmes and Szechi (1993), appendices.

32. NLS MS 17514, f. 55 for strength of Jacobite recruitment in Edinburgh and Stirling shires; Mary Ingram, *A Jacobite Stronghold of the Church* (Edinburgh: R. Grant & Son, 1907), 33; Forbes (1895).

33. McCann (1963), 76 (burgh records); Rosebery (1890), 3ff.; Taylers (1928), passim; *The Miscellany of the Spalding Club*, vol. 1 (1841), 353, 357 for the behaviour of Aberdeen Grammar School's masters.

34. W. B. Blaikie (1916), 129; *The Miscellany of the Spalding Club*, vol. 1 (1841), 363 and passim; McCann (1963), 75, 77 for forcing figures.

35. Cf. Stevenson (1973), 71; 'The Aberdeen Doctors', *Aberdeen Notes & Queries* 4 (1911), 286–7; 290–1; 297–9; Furgol (1990), 61, 133, 165, 195, 220, 296ff., 378. For the militia raised after Cumberland's departure, see Blaikie (1916), 160; Taylers (1928), 418ff.; *The Miscellany of the Spalding Club* vol. 1 (1841), 356.

36. Taylers (1928), 8 for dislike of the malt tax; also 14, 115ff., 288, 406; Blaikie (1916), 122 and 130–1 for malt tax; NLS MS 3787 for the Order Book of the Appin Regiment; Rosebery (1890), passim; NLS MS 17522 and Livingstone (1984) for figures.

37. Furgol (1990), 22, 271, 308 and passim.

38. NLS MS 17522, ff. 31–4; NLS MS 17514, f. 109 for Forfarshire deserters.

39. Lockhart (1989), 217 (actually 'those loyal shyres [Angus and Mearns]'); NLS MS 17514, f. 87; NLS MS 17522, f. 35ff.; Mackintosh (1914), 90 confirms.

40. NLS MS 17522, f. 35ff. for assessments of the rebellious; 56, 83, 85, 87 for Stonehaven support; MS 17523, ff. 197–8 for sympathisers in Stonehaven; NLS MS 280 for behaviour of the governor at Stonehaven in 1715 and 1745; *Atholl Correspondence* (1840), 96–7; NLS MS 17514, f. 57 for Dalkeith intelligence.

41. Cf. Furgol (1990), 32.

42. McCann (1963), 39–55, 197 for Jacobite recruitment and motivation. For Jacobite strength among the Perthshire lairds, see T. L. Kingston Oliphant, *The Jacobite Lairds of Gask*, The Grampian Club (London: Charles Griffin and Co., 1870), 102; *Atholl Correspondence* (1840), passim; NLS MS 17522.

43. NLS MS 17522, ff. 45, 55 for Jacobite strength in Anstruther and Fraserburgh; Furgol (1990), 114, 135, 137; McCann (1963), ix for St Andrews, 95–6, 108 for social background.

44. McCann (1963), ix–x.

45. NLS MS 17522, f. 36ff. for recruitment in the south-west; Furgol (1990), 45, 51, 62, 134, 141 and passim.
46. NLS MS 17514, f. 231; NLS MS 17522, ff. 111–15, 128ff.
47. Taylers (1936), 122 for Peterhead's sympathies in the earlier rising; Patten's list. Cf. Kyd (1952), 8ff. for the principles underlying the figures given.
48. Robertson (1985), 110–11 for the size of the militia; 'Assessment for the Execution of the Press Act', NLS MS 17505, f. 98; Lenman (1984) 193; John Childs, 'The Restoration Army 1660–1702' in David Chandler (gen. ed.); Ian Beckett (associate ed.), *The Oxford Illustrated History of the British Army* (Oxford and New York: Oxford University Press, 1994), 48–68; also David Chandler, 'The Great Captain-General', in ibid. (1994), 75 and Alan J. Guy, 'The Army of the Four Georges, 1714–1783', 103.
49. *Atholl Correspondence* (1840) gives ample detail of the difficulty in finding men to raise men; Frank McLynn (1988), 149 for the sending home of the Camerons.
50. McCann (1963), xi, 8; NLS MS 1498, f. 1r for the size of units in Mar's army at Perth.
51. McCann (1963), xiff., Livingstone (1984). For Highland numbers in 1715, see Taylers (1936), 39ff.; Baynes (1970), 59ff.
52. Campbell (1985 (1965)), 7; McCann (1963), 95–6, 108; Taylers (1928), passim; NLS MS 17522, f. 10ff. for social background; f. 35 ('A list of Persons in and about the District of Montrose Said to be Concerned in the Wicked and Unnatural Rebellion'); MS 17522, f. 38 for the social class of Aberdeen recruits; f. 56 for those claiming forcing in Stonehaven; ff. 82, 83, 85, 87 for their social background; Livingstone (1984) for social make-up of the Forfarshires.
53. NLS MS 17522, ff. 10ff., 35, 38, 50ff., 82ff. and passim.
54. See Paul Monod, 'The Politics of Matrimony', in Eveline Cruickshanks and Jeremy Black (eds), *The Jacobite Challenge* (Edinburgh: John Donald, 1988), 24–41.
55. Livingstone (1984), passim.
56. For Jacobite smuggling and criminality, see Frank McLynn, *Crime and Punishment in Eighteenth-Century England* (London: Routledge, 1989); Paul Monod, 'Dangerous Merchandise: Smuggling, Jacobitism and Commercial Culture in Southeast England', *Journal of British Studies* 30:2 (1991), 150–82.
57. NLS MS 98, f. 39; Wood (1989), 92, 102, 106.
58. Farquhar (1894), 161, 171, 199 for the decline in Episcopal clergy and status of licensed congregations.

Chapter 3

1. Lockhart (1989), 252; F. W. Robertson, 'Re-Appraising the Forty-five', *Scots Independent* (April 1944), 4; Lindsay Paterson, *The Autonomy of Modern Scotland* (Edinburgh: Edinburgh University Press, 1994); Charles Edward Stuart's memorandum quoted in John Gibson, *Lochiel of the '45* (Edinburgh: Edinburgh University Press, 1994), 157.

2. Cf. the work of Bruce Lenman, Frank McLynn, Jeremy Black, J. C. D. Clark, Eveline Cruickshanks and Paul Monod among others.

3. Cf. Murray G. H. Pittock, 'From Edinburgh to London: Scottish Court Writing and 1603', in *Studies in Voltaire and the Eighteenth Century*, forthcoming.

4. Cf. Hugh Ouston, 'York in Edinburgh: James VII and the Patronage of Learning in Scotland, 1679–1688', in John Dwyer, Roger Mason and Alexander Murdoch (eds), *New Perspectives on the Politics and Culture of Early Modern Scotland* (Edinburgh: John Donald, n.d. (c. 1983)), 133–55.

5. P. W. J. Riley, *The Union of England and Scotland* (Manchester: Manchester University Press, 1978), 204–5; cf. Pittock (1991), 25–40; Colonel James Allardyce (ed.), *Historical Papers Relating to the Jacobite Period 1699–1750* (Aberdeen: New Spalding Club, 1895), vol. 1, pp. 177, 188–9.

6. Frank McLynn, 'An Eighteenth-Century Scots Republic? – An Unlikely Project from Absolutist France', *Scottish Historical Review* 59 (1980), 177–81; Gibson (1994), 163; D. H. MacNeill, 'Scottish and English Jacobites', *Scots Independent* 167 (April, 1941).

7. John Gibson, *Playing the Scottish Card* (Edinburgh: Edinburgh University Press, 1988), 75ff.; '"Scotland's Ruine!": The Memoirs of George Lockhart of Carnwath', ed. Daniel Szechi with an Introduction by Paul Scott (Aberdeen: Association for Scottish Literary Studies, forthcoming) for Presbyterian nationalist sentiments on James; Szechi (ed.), *Letters of George Lockhart of Carnwath* (1989), 141. These are also cited in William Donaldson, 'The Jacobite Song in 18th and Early 19th Century Scotland', unpublished Ph.D. thesis (University of Aberdeen, 1974), 45.

8. Cited in Rev. W. H. Langhorne, *Reminiscences* (Edinburgh: David Douglas, 1893), 9.

9. James's declaration, cited in Taylers (1936), 123, 311–14; *A Fragment of a Memoir of Field-Marshal James Keith, Written by Himself 1714–1734* (Edinburgh: Spalding Club, 1843), 11 for taxation on the old Scots footing; Sinclair (1858), 2.

10. Linda Colley, *In Defiance of Oligarchy* (Cambridge: Cambridge University Press, 1982), 105 for the Whigging of the bench of bishops; cf. Pittock (1994), Introduction and following, for the Nonjurors and 'British Catholicism'.

11. Forbes (1895) vol. 1, p. 63 for Cappoch's last words; NLS MS 1012 for Garden's sermon; Riley (1978), 282.

12. William Gillies, 'Gaelic Songs of the 'Forty-Five', *Scottish Studies* 30 (1991), 46; S. Bruce and S. Yearley, 'The Social Construction of Tradition: The Restoration Portraits and the Kings of Scotland', in David McCrone, Stephen Kendrick and Pat Shaw (eds), *The Making of Scotland: Nation, Culture and Social Change* (Edinburgh: Edinburgh University Press and British Sociological Association, 1989), 180, 183; Roger A. Mason, 'Scotching the Brut', in idem (ed.), *Scotland and England 1286–1815* (Edinburgh: John Donald, 1986), 60.

13. *Scotland's Glory and Her Shame* (1745, 1786), discussed in Pittock (1991), 65; cf. Taylers (1936), 129; also cf. NLS MS 17498, f. 145 ('A speech without doors upon the present state of the Nation'), for anti-Union feeling in Scotland, particularly f. 2r; Rev. J. B. Cronin, *History of the Episcopal Church in the Diocese of Moray* (London: Skeffington & Son, 1889).

14. Szechi (ed.), *Letters of George Lockhart of Carnwath* (1989), xxxiii–xxxiv, 182ff. for Usagers controversy; also pp. 217, 262; NLS MS 1498, 6 for James's letter; McCann (1963), 138 for anti-Episcopal action in 1716; Gibson (1988), 74.

15. For the shifting ground of Williamite Tories, cf. H. T. Dickinson, *Liberty and Property* (London: Edward Arnold, 1977); Lord Forbes of Pitsligo, in Aberdeen University Library MS 2740/4/18/1. See also Murray G. H. Pittock, 'Jacobitism in the North-East: The Pitsligo Papers in Aberdeen University Library', in J. J. Carter and J. H. Pittock (eds), *Aberdeen in the Enlightenment* (Aberdeen: Aberdeen University Press, 1987), 69–76.

16. Forbes (1895), vols 1 and 2; cf. Farquhar (1894), 171–99 and passim.

17. Forbes (1895), vol. 3; Farquhar (1894), 161; The Very Rev. W. Perry, *The Oxford Movement in Scotland* (Cambridge: Cambridge University Press, 1933), 36; Alexander, 4th Lord Forbes of Pitsligo, *Thoughts Concerning Man's Condition and Duties in This Life, and His Hopes in the World to Come*, 4th edn, with a Biographical Sketch by Lord Medwyn and a Review by Sir Walter Scott (Edinburgh and London: William Blackwood, 1854), 37; xliii in the 1829 edition for comment on the penal laws against Episcopacy.

18. Lenman (1980); Monod (1989); Pittock (1994); cf. also the work of Breandan Ó Buachalla.

19. Langhorne (1893), 12; F. W. Freeman, 'Robert Fergusson: Pastoral and Politics at Mid Century', in Andrew Hook (ed.), *The History of Scottish Literature Volume 2* (Aberdeen: Aberdeen University Press, 1987), 141–56; Nelson S. Bushnell, *William Hamilton of Bangour: Poet and Jacobite* (Aberdeen: Aberdeen University Press, 1957), 83.
20. Rebellious Pieces, NLS MS 98; Pittock (1994), introduction; chs 2 and 4.
21. Cf. Murray G. H. Pittock, 'New Jacobite Songs of the Forty-five', *Studies in Voltaire and the Eighteenth Century* 267 (1989), 1–75.
22. Pittock (1994), chs 2, 4.
23. Ibid.
24. Pittock (1991), ch. 2; William Donaldson (1988), ch. 1.

Chapter 4

1. Thomas Richards, *The Commodity Culture of Victorian England* (Stanford: Stanford University Press, 1990), 88; George Rosie, 'Museumry and the Heritage Industry', in Donnachie and Whatley (eds) (1992), 166; also Donnachie and Whatley (eds), 2.
2. Pittock (1991), ch. 3, especially 88–9; cf. Monod (1989).
3. Richards (1990), 90; Bruce Lenman (1984) for the tartanisation of the British Army; John Dwyer and Alexander Murdoch, 'Paradigms and Politics: Manners, Morals and the Rise of Henry Dundas, 1770–1784', in Dwyer, Mason and Murdoch (eds) (1983), 217.
4. Steve Sweeney-Turner, 'Music Fyne: More Parcels of Rogues', *Cencrastus* 50 (1994/95), 29.
5. Carolyn Williams, seminar paper in British Society for Eighteenth-Century Studies annual seminar 1995 ('The '45: Reality and Representations'), London, January 1995. Burke's famous passage and denigration of 'sophisters and oeconomists' comes, of course, from his prophetic *Reflections on the Revolution in France* (1790).
6. Cf. the emphasis on Jacobite *artefacts* in the 1995–6 commemorations and their exhibitions at Glasgow and Culloden. Cf. also Richards's statement (Richards (1990), 17) that 'the Great Exhibition of 1851 had at its root a single conception: that all human life and culture could be fully represented by exhibiting manufactured articles'.
7. Cf. Pittock (1991), ch. 4.
8. L. M. G., 'The "Elusive Gael" – and the Highland Delusion', *Scots Independent* (1928), 94–5.
9. John Springhall, '"Up Guards and at Them!": British Imperialism and Popular Art, 1880–1914', in John M. Mackenzie (ed.), *Imperialism and Popular Culture* (Manchester: Manchester University Press, 1986), 50; Paul Greenhalgh, *Imperial Vistas* (Manchester: Manchester University Press, 1988), 64.

10. A. C. MacDonell, *Lays of the Heather: Poems* (London: Elliot Stock, 1896), 5–6, 33.
11. Osmond (1988), 191, 246. Michael Fry's forthcoming book on 'Scottish Empire' promises to redress the balance somewhat.

List of the Jacobite Units in the Rising of 1745

The Aberdeen Battalion (Stoneywood's)
(The Aboyne Battalion)
The Appin Regiment
The Atholl Brigade (four battalions)
Avochie's Strathbogie Battalion
Balmoral Battalion
Bannerman of Elsick's Mearns Battalion
Cameron of Lochiel's Regiment
Chisholm of Strathglass's (one to two companies)
Duke of Perth's Regiment (two battalions)
Earl of Cromartie's Regiment
The Edinburgh Regiment
Forfarshire Regiment (two battalions)
Frasers of Lovat
Viscount Frendraught's Aberdeen unit (one to two companies)
Glenbucket's Regiment
Grante's Artillery
MacDonald of Clanranald's
MacDonald of Glencoe's (two to three companies)

MacDonell of Glengarry's (two battalions)
MacDonell of Keppoch's
MacGregor of Glengyle's
Mackinnon's
Lady Mackintosh's
MacLachlan's and MacLean's (two battalions)
MacLeod of Raasay (one company)
Macpherson of Cluny's
Manchester Regiment
Monaltrie's Battalion
The Royal Scots (French service)
Stapleton's piquets from the Irish Brigade

Cavalry

Baggot's Troop of Hussars
Balmerino's Troop of Lifeguards
Elcho's Troop of Lifeguards
Fitzjames's cavalry squadron
Kilmarnock's Grenadiers
Lord Pitsligo's Horse
The Perthshire Horse squadron (Gask's and Lanerick's Troops)

Bibliography

Primary Sources

Manuscripts

Aberdeen University Library MS 2740/4/18/1/1–18 (Pitsligo Papers).
National Library of Scotland ACC 8611.
NLS ACC 8326 ('Receipt Cess for Land Hadington 1745').
NLS ACC 9202 (Jacobite songs).
National Library of Scotland Advocates MS 19.3.28.
NLS Advocates MS 22.2.20.
NLS Advocates MS 23.3.26 (Eaglescarnie Papers).
NLS Advocates MS 23.3.28 (Eaglescarnie Papers).
NLS Advocates MS 23.3.29 ('Peter Lindsay's (autograph) Notes of Orders &c At Perth, Nairn House, & Dunkeld March 15–Ap 5 1746').
NLS Advocates MS 23.3.30.
NLS Advocates MS 28.1.6.
NLS Advocates MS 82.9.2.
NLS Deposit 344/1 (Transcript of 'Thomas Muir of Huntershill' by George Pratt Insh).
NLS MS 98 (Irish Brigade recruiting in Scotland).
NLS MS 280 (Behaviour of Governor at Stonehaven in 1715 and 1745).
NLS MS 290 (list of Jacobite officers in 1745 compiled by W. B. Blaikie).
NLS MS 293 ('An Impartial and Genuine List of the Ladys on the Whig . . . or . . . Jacobite Partie').
NLS MS 300 ('Rebellion – An MS. poem in Five books').

NLS MS 874 ('Information of A. B. to J. C. regarding Jacobite plotting in Scotland in 1715').

NLS MS 1012 (sermon of the Reverend Professor James Garden, New Church of Aberdeen, 1715).

NLS MS 1498 ('List of the King's Army'; letter of James VIII from Urbino (1717)).

NLS MS 2092.

NLS MS 2910 ('Choice Poems &c on Several Occasions preceeding [sic] 1745').

NLS MS 2960 ('Jacobite song, from the recitation of Mrs. McLehose').

NLS MS 3114.

NLS MS 3142.

NLS MS 3740 (unrest in Northern Ireland, 1704–5).

NLS MS 3787 (Order Book of Appin's Regiment).

NLS MS 6290.

NLS MS 8027.

NLS MS 16971, f. 1 (Saltoun Papers: conduct of Pelham in the Rising).

NLS MS 17498.

NLS MS 17503.

NLS MS 17505.

NLS MS 17514 ('Intelligence Reports on the Rebellion').

NLS MS 17522 ('Miscellaneous Documents').

NLS MS 17523.

NLS MS 17524.

NLS MS 17525.

NLS MS 21834 ('Jacobite Songs Written in Ceylon in 1866 by H. Davidson').

Printed

An Account of the Proceedings of the Meeting of the Estates in Scotland. London, 1689.

Æneas and His Two Sons. London: J. Oldcastle, 1745/6.

Allardyce, Colonel James (ed.), *Historical Papers Relating to the Jacobite Period 1699–1750*, vols 1 and 2. Aberdeen: New Spalding Club, 1895/6.

Anderson, James, *Scotland Independent.* Edinburgh, 1705.

Ashton, John, *Chapbooks of the Eighteenth Century.* With Facsimiles, Notes and Introduction. London: Chatto & Windus, 1882.

'LORD BELHAVEN'S SPEECH IN PARLIAMENT' to which is Subjoined *'BELHAVEN'S VISION': A Poem.* Edinburgh: A. Robertson, 1766.

Bibliography

Blaikie, Walter Biggar, *Origins of the 'Forty-Five: And Other Papers Relating to that Rising*. Edinburgh: T. & A. Constable, 1916.

Blood, Bindon and James MacKnight (eds), *Memoirs of Sir Ewan Cameron of Locheill*. Edinburgh: Abbotsford Club, 1842.

Burton and Laing (eds), *Jacobite Correspondence of The Atholl Family During the Rebellion, 1745–46*. Edinburgh: Abbotsford Club, 1840.

Chambers, Robert, *History of the Rebellion of 1745–6*. New edition. London and Edinburgh: W. & R. Chambers, 1869.

Craig, Sir Thomas, *Scotland's Soveraignty Asserted*. London, 1695.

Dalton, Charles, *The Scots Army 1661–1688 With Memoirs of the Commanders-in-Chief*. 2 parts. London: Eyre & Spottiswoode Ltd; Edinburgh: William Brown, 1909.

A Discourse of the Necessity and Seasonableness of an unanimous Address for Dissolving the Union. n.p., 1715.

Elcho, Lord, *A Short Account of the Affairs of Scotland in the Years 1744, 1745, 1746*. Ed. Hon. Evan Charteris. Edinburgh: David Douglas, 1907.

Forbes, Alexander, 4th Lord Forbes of Pitsligo, *Thoughts Concerning Man's Condition and Duties in this Life, and His Hopes in the World to Come*. Edinburgh: William Whyte; London: Longman & Co. and J. Nisbet, 1829. Also 4th (1854) edition, 'with a Biographical Sketch of the Author by Lord Medwyn and a Review by Sir Walter Scott'. Edinburgh and London: William Blackwood.

Forbes, Bishop Robert, *The Lyon in Mourning*. Ed. Henry Paton. Scottish History Society, 3 vols. Edinburgh: Edinburgh University Press, 1895.

A Fragment of a Memoir of Field-Marshal James Keith, Written by Himself 1714–1734. Edinburgh: Spalding Club, 1843.

'The Highlanders at Macclesfield in 1745'. *Scottish Historical Review* 5 (1908), 285–96.

A King and No King. London: S. Popping, 1716.

Kyd, James Gray, CBE FRSE FFA (ed.), *Scottish Population Statistics*. Publications of the Scottish History Society, 3rd Series, vol. 44. Edinburgh: T. & A. Constable, 1952.

The Laws and Acts Made in the First Parliament of Our most High and Dread Sovereign James VII. Ed. George, Viscount Tarbet. Edinburgh, 1731.

List of Persons Concerned in the Rebellion Transmitted to the Commissioners of Excise by the Several Supervisors in Scotland in Obedience to a General Letter of 7th May 1746 and a Supplementary List with Evidences to Prove the Same, with a Preface by the Earl of Rosebery and Annotations by the Rev. Walter Macleod. Publications of the Scottish History Society, vol. 8. Edinburgh: Edinburgh University Press, 1890.

Livingstone of Bachuil, Alastair et al. (eds), *Muster Roll of Prince Edward Stuart's Army 1745–46*. With an introduction by Bruce Lenman. Aberdeen: Aberdeen University Press, 1984.

Mackenzie, Sir George, *A Defence of the Antiquity of the Royal-Line of Scotland*. London: printed for R. C., 1685.

Millar, A. H. (ed.), *Scottish Forfeited Estates Papers*. Scottish History Society, vol. 57. Edinburgh: University Press, T. & A. Constable, 1909.

Miscellany of the Scottish History Society. Scottish History Society, 3rd series, vol. 4. Edinburgh: EdinburghUniversity Press and T. & A. Constable, 1926.

The Miscellany of the Spalding Club, vol. 1. Aberdeen, 1841.

The Miscellany of the Spalding Club, vol. 2. Aberdeen, 1842.

The Miscellany of the Spalding Club, vol. 4. Aberdeen, 1849.

Musa Latina Aberdoniensis. Ed. Sir William Duguid Geddes LL.D. (vols 1 & 2) and William Keith Leasle (vol. 3). Aberdeen: New Spalding Club, 1892, 1895 and 1910.

Perceval, Milton (ed.), *Political Ballads Illustrating the Administration of Sir Robert Walpole*. Volume 8 of Oxford Historical and Literary Studies. Oxford: Clarendon Press, 1916.

Scott, Andrew Murray (ed.), 'Letters of John Graham of Claverhouse'. Scottish History Society 5:3, *Miscellany* 11. Edinburgh: Scottish History Society, 1990.

Seton, Sir Bruce of Ancrum, Bart, and Jean Gordon Arnot, *The Prisoners of the '45*. Scottish History Society, 3 vols. Edinburgh: Edinburgh University Press, 1928/9.

Sinclair, John, Master of, *Memoirs of the Insurrection in Scotland in 1715*. Ed. messrs MacKnight and Lang, with notes by Sir Walter Scott, Bart. Edinburgh: Abbotsford Club, 1858.

Smythe, George (ed.), *Letters of John Grahame of Claverhouse Viscount of Dundee with Illustrative Documents*. Bannatyne Club. Edinburgh: James Ballantyne & Co., 1843.

Szechi, Daniel (ed.), *Letters of George Lockhart of Carnwath*. Scottish History Society 5:2. Edinburgh: Scottish History Society, 1989.

—— (ed.), '"Scotland's Ruine!": The Memoirs of George Lockhart of Carnwath', with an Introduction by Paul Scott. Aberdeen: Association for Scottish Literary Studies, forthcoming (read in MS).

Tayler, Alistair and Henrietta Tayler (eds), *The Jacobite Cess Roll for the County of Aberdeen in 1715*. Aberdeen: Third Spalding Club, 1932.

Villpone: Or, Remarks on Some Proceedings in Scotland. n.p., 1707.

Secondary Sources

'The Aberdeen Doctors'. *Aberdeen Journal Notes & Queries* 4 (1911), 286–7, 290–1, 297–9.

Aberdeen Journal Notes & Queries 1–5, 7 (1908–12/14).

Adamson, Ian, *The Identity of Ulster: The Land, the Language and the People*. Ulster: Ian Adamson, 1982.

Anderson, Benedict, *Imagined Communities: Reflections on the Origin and Spread of Nationalism*. London: Verso, 1983.

Ankersmit, F. R. (ed.), *Knowing and Telling History: The Anglo-Saxon Debate*. History and Theory Wesleyan University: Studies in the Philosophy of History, 1986.

Anson, Peter F., *Underground Catholicism in Scotland 1622–1878*. Montrose: Standard Press, 1970.

Ash, Marinell, *The Strange Death of Scottish History*. Edinburgh: Ramsay Head Press, 1980.

—— 'William Wallace and Robert the Bruce: The Life and Death of a National Myth', in Raphael Samuel and Paul Thompson (eds), *The Myths We Live By*. London and New York: Routledge, 1990, 83–94.

Baynes, John, *The Jacobite Rising of 1715*. London: Cassell, 1970.

Beddard, Robert (ed.), *The Revolutions of 1688: The Andrew Browning Lectures*. Oxford: Clarendon Press, 1991.

Behre, Govan, 'Sweden and the Rising of 1745'. *Scottish Historical Review* 51 (1972), 148–71.

—— 'Two Swedish Expeditions to Rescue Prince Charles'. *Scottish Historical Review* 59 (1980), 140–53.

Benson, Lee, *Towards the Scientific Study of History*. Philadelphia, New York, Toronto: J. B. Lippincott & Co., 1972.

Birkenhead, The Rt Hon. The Earl of, *Turning Points in History*. London: Hutchinson & Co., n.d.

Black, Jeremy (ed.), *Britain in the Age of Walpole*. London: Macmillan, 1984.

—— *Culloden and the '45*. Stroud: Alan Sutton, 1990.

Blaikie, W. B., 'The Highlanders at Macclesfield in 1745'. *Scottish Historical Review* 6 (1909), 225–44.

Blaikie Murdoch, W. G., *The Spirit of Jacobite Loyalty*. Edinburgh: William Brown, 1907.

Braudel, Fernand, *On History*. Tr. Sarah Matthews. London: Weidenfeld and Nicolson, 1980.

Broad, John, 'Whigs and Deer-Stealers in Other Guises: A Return to the Origins of the Black Act'. *Past and Present* 119 (1988), 56–72.

Brown, Iain Gordon, 'Modern Rome and Ancient Caledonia: The

Union and the Politics of Scottish Culture', in Andrew Hook (ed.), *The History of Scottish Literature Volume 2* (4 vols, gen. ed. Cairns Craig). Aberdeen: Aberdeen University Press, 1987, 33–50.

Brown, P. Hume, *The Legislative Union of England and Scotland*. Oxford: Clarendon Press, 1914.

Broxap, Henry, *The Later Non-Jurors*. Cambridge: Cambridge University Press, 1924.

Bruce, S. and S. Yearley, 'The Social Construction of Tradition: The Restoration Portraits and the Kings of Scotland', in David McCrone, Stephen Kendrick and Pat Shaw (eds), *The Making of Scotland: Nation, Culture and Social Change*. Edinburgh: Edinburgh University Press and British Sociological Association, 1989, 175–88.

Buchan, David, *The Ballad and the Folk*. London: Routledge & Kegan Paul, 1972.

Burnet, George R., *The Story of Quakerism in Scotland 1650–1850* with an Epilogue on the Period 1850–1950 by William H. Marwick. London: James Clarke, 1952.

Burton, I. F. and A. N. Newman, 'Sir John Cope: Promotion in the Eighteenth-Century Army'. *English Historical Review* 78 (1963), 655–68.

Bushnell, Nelson S., *William Hamilton of Bangour: Poet and Jacobite*. Aberdeen: Aberdeen University Press, 1957.

Butterfield, Herbert, *The Whig Interpretation of History*. London: G. Bell & Sons, 1931.

Campbell, R. H., *Scotland Since 1707: The Rise of an Industrial Society*. 2nd edn. Edinburgh: John Donald, 1985 (1965).

Carmichael, Elizabeth K., 'Jacobitism in the Scottish Commission of the Peace, 1707–1760'. *Scottish Historical Review* 58 (1979), 58–69.

Carr, E. H., *What is History?* 2nd edn. London: Penguin, 1990 (1987).

Carter, J. J. and J. H. Pittock (eds), *Aberdeen and the Enlightenment*. Aberdeen: Aberdeen University Press, 1987.

Cassell's History of the British People. 7 vols. London: The Waverley Book Co., 1923.

Cencrastus, 1988–94.

Chandler, David (general editor); Beckett, Ian (associate editor), *The Oxford Illustrated History of the British Army*. Oxford and New York: Oxford University Press, 1994.

Chandler, David, 'The Great Captain-General', in idem (gen. ed.), *The Oxford Illustrated History of the British Army*. Oxford and New York: Oxford University Press, 1994, 69–91.

Chesterton, G. K., *A Short History of England*. London: Chatto & Windus, 1917.

Childs, John, *The Army, James II and the Glorious Revolution*.

Manchester: Manchester University Press, 1980.

—— 'The Restoration Army 1660–1702', in David Chandler (gen. ed.), *The Oxford Illustrated History of the British Army*. Oxford and New York: Oxford University Press, 1994, 48–68.

Churchill, Sir Winston S., *A History of the English-Speaking Peoples*. 7 vols. London: Cassell and Company Ltd, 1957.

Clark, Sir George, *English History: A Survey*. Oxford: Clarendon Press, 1971.

Clarke, Tristram, 'The Williamite Episcopalians and the Glorious Revolution in Scotland'. *Scottish Church History Society Records* XXIV (1992), 33–52.

Clyne, Norval, *The Scottish Jacobites and their Poetry*. Aberdeen, 1887.

Cohen, Sande, *Historical Culture: On the Recording of an Academic Discipline*. Berkeley, Los Angeles and London: University of California Press, 1986.

Colley, Linda, *In Defiance of Oligarchy*. Cambridge: Cambridge University Press, 1985 (1982).

—— *Britons*. New Haven: Yale University Press, 1992.

Colls, Robert and Philip Dodd (eds), *Englishness: Politics and Culture 1880–1920*. London: Croom Helm, 1986.

Corp, Edward T. (ed.), *L'autre exil: Les Jacobites en France au début du XVIIIe siècle*. Les Presses du Languedoc, 1993.

Cronin, Rev. J. B., *History of the Episcopal Church in the Diocese of Moray*. London: Skeffington & Son, 1889.

Cruickshanks, Eveline and Jeremy Black (eds), *The Jacobite Challenge*. Edinburgh: John Donald, 1988.

Daiches, David, *Robert Fergusson*. Scottish Writers Series. Edinburgh: Scottish Academic Press, 1982.

Dance, E. H., 'Bias in History Teaching and Textbooks', in Otto-Ernst Schuddehopf et al., *History Teaching and History Textbook Revision*. Strasbourg: Centre for Cultural Co-operation of the Council of Europe, 1967, 73ff.

Dicey, A. V. and Robert S. Rait, *Thoughts on the Union between England and Scotland*. London: Macmillan, 1920.

Dickinson, H. T., 'The Eighteenth-Century Debate on the Glorious Revolution'. *History* 61 (1976), 28–45.

—— *Liberty and Property*. London: Edward Arnold, 1977.

—— *Caricatures and the Constitution 1760–1832*. The English Satirical Print 1600–1832. Cambridge: Chadwyck-Healey, 1986.

Donaldson, Gordon, *Scottish Church History*. Edinburgh: Scottish Academic Press, 1985.

Donaldson, William, 'The Jacobite Song in 18th and Early 19th Century

Scotland'. Unpublished Ph.D. thesis. University of Aberdeen, 1974.

—— *The Jacobite Song*. Aberdeen: Aberdeen University Press, 1988.

Donnachie, Ian and Christopher Whatley (eds). *The Manufacture of Scottish History*. Edinburgh: Polygon, 1992.

Dwyer, John, Roger A. Mason and Alexander Murdoch (eds), *New Perspectives on the Politics and Culture of Early Modern Scotland*. Edinburgh: John Donald, n.d. (c. 1983).

Dwyer, John and Alexander Murdoch, 'Paradigms and Politics: Manners, Morals and the Rise of Henry Dundas, 1770–1784', in John Dwyer, Roger A. Mason and Alexander Murdoch (eds), *New Perspectives on the Politics and Culture of Early Modern Scotland*. Edinburgh: John Donald, n.d. (c. 1983).

Ellis, Peter Berresford, *The Celtic Revolution*. Talybont: Y Lolfa, 1985.

Elton, G. R., *Political History: Principles and Practice*. Allen Lane: Penguin Press, 1970.

Farquhar, Rev. Canon George, *The Episcopal History of Perth*. Perth: James H. Jackson, 1894.

Feiling, Keith, *A History of England From the Coming of the English to 1918*. London: Macmillan, 1950.

Ferguson, William, *Scotland: 1689 to the Present*. The Edinburgh History of Scotland Volume 4. Edinburgh: Oliver and Boyd, 1968.

—— 'Imperial Crowns: A Neglected Facet of the Background to the Treaty of Union of 1707'. *Scottish Historical Review* 53 (1974), 22–44.

Firth, C. H., 'Ballads on the Bishops' Wars, 1638–1640'. Scottish Historical Review 3 (1906), 257–73.

—— 'Ballads Illustrating the Relations of England and Scotland during the Seventeenth Century'. *Scottish Historical Review* 6 (1909), 113–28.

—— 'A New Year's Gift for the Whigs'. Ibid. (1909a), 245–7.

—— 'Jacobite Songs'. *Scottish Historical Review* 8 (1911), 251–7.

—— 'Two Ballads on Viscount Dundee'. Ibid. (1911a), 361–5.

Flinn, Michael et al. (eds), *Scottish Population History from the 17th century to the 1930s*. Cambridge: Cambridge University Press, 1977.

Fraser, Duncan, *Montrose (before 1700)*. Montrose: Standard Press, 1970.

Freeman, F. W., 'Robert Fergusson: Pastoral and Politics at Mid Century', in Andrew Hook (ed.), *The History of Scottish Literature Volume 2* 4 vols, gen. ed. Cairns Craig). Aberdeen: Aberdeen University Press, 1987, 141–56.

Fry, Michael, 'The Whig Interpretation of Scottish History', in Ian Donnachie and Christopher Whatley (eds), *The Manufacture of Scottish History*. Edinburgh: Polygon, 1992, 72–89.

Fryer, Mary Beacock, *Allan Maclean: Jacobite General*. Toronto: Dundurn Press, 1987.

Furgol, Edward M., *A Regimental History of the Covenanting Armies, 1639–1651*. Edinburgh: John Donald, 1990.

L.M.G., 'The "Elusive Gael" – and the Highland Delusion'. *Scots Independent* II(6) (1928), 94–5.

Gardiner, Samuel R., DCL LLD, *A Student's History of England from Earliest Times to the Death of King Edward VII*. New edn. London, New York, Bombay and Calcutta: Longmans, Green & Co., 1910.

Gellner, Ernest, *Nations and Nationalism*. Oxford: Basil Blackwell, 1983.

—— *Plough, Sword and Book: The Structure of Human History*. London and Glasgow: Paladin, 1991 (1988).

Gibson, John, *Playing the Scottish Card*. Edinburgh: Edinburgh University Press, 1988.

—— *Lochiel of the '45*. Edinburgh: Edinburgh University Press, 1994.

Gillespie, Raymond, 'The Irish Protestants and James II'. *Irish Historical Studies* XXVIII:10 (1992), 124–33.

Gillies, William, 'Gaelic Songs of the 'Forty-Five'. *Scottish Studies* 30 (1991), 19–58.

Gossman, Lionel, 'Towards a Rational Historiography'. *Transactions of the American Philosophical Society* 79:3 (1989), 1–68.

Gray, W. Forbes and James H. Jamieson, *A Short History of Haddington*. East Lothian Antiquarian and Field Naturalists' Society. Edinburgh: Neill & Co., 1944.

Green, J. R., *A Short History of the English People*. London: Macmillan and Co., 1875.

Greenhalgh, Paul, *Ephemeral Vistas: The Expositions Universelles, Great Exhibitions and World's Fairs, 1851–1939*. Manchester: Manchester University Press, 1988.

Guy, Alan J., 'The Army of the Four Georges, 1714–1783', in David Chandler (gen. ed.), *The Oxford Illustrated History of the British Army*. Oxford and New York: Oxford University Press, 1994, 92–110.

Gwynn, Robin D., 'James II in the Light of his Treatment of Huguenot Refugees in England, 1685–1686'. *English Historical Review* 92 (1977), 820–33.

Hallam, Henry, *The Constitutional History of England: From the Accession of Henry VII to the Death of George II*. 8th edn. 3 vols. London: John Murray, 1867 (1827).

Harvie, Christopher, *Scotland and Nationalism: Scottish Society and Politics 1707–1994*. 2nd edn. London and New York: Routledge, 1994.

Heeks, Peter, 'Myth, History, and Theory'. *History and Theory* 33:1 (1994), 1–19.

Henderson, G. D., *Mystics of the North East*. Aberdeen: Third Spalding Club, 1934.

Henning, Basil Duke, Archibald S. Foord and Barbara L. Matthias (eds) *Crises in English History 1066–1945*. New York: Holt, Rinehart & Winston, 1961 (1949).

Hepburn, A. C., *Minorities in History*. London: Edward Arnold, 1978.

Hewitt, D. S. and J. H. Alexander (eds), *Scott in Carnival*. Aberdeen: Association for Scottish Literary Studies, 1993.

Hill, Christopher, *Puritanism and Revolution*. London: Secker & Warburg, 1958.

—— *Some Intellectual Consequences of the English Revolution*. London: Weidenfeld & Nicolson, 1980.

The Collected Essays of Christopher Hill Volume 1: Writing and Revolution in 17th Century England. Brighton: The Harvester Press, 1985.

Hill, James Michael, *Celtic Warfare 1595–1763*. Edinburgh: John Donald, 1986.

Hill, Patricia Kneas, *The Oglethorpe Ladies*. Atlanta: Cherokee, 1977.

Hobsbawm, Eric and Terence Ranger (eds), *The Invention of Tradition*. Cambridge: Cambridge University Press, 1983.

Hogg, James, *The Jacobite Relics*. 2 vols. Edinburgh, 1819/21.

Holmes, Geoffrey, *The Trial of Doctor Sacheverell*. London: Eyre Methuen, 1973.

Holmes, Geoffrey and Daniel Szechi, *The Age of Oligarchy: Pre-industrial Britain 1722–1783*. London and New York: Longman, 1993.

Hook, Andrew (ed.), *The History of Scottish Literature Volume 2*. 4 vols, gen. ed. Cairns Craig. Aberdeen: Aberdeen University Press, 1987.

Hopkins, Paul, *Glencoe and the End of the Highland War*. Edinburgh: John Donald, 1986.

The Independent, 5 August 1993, p. 4: for John Major's April 1993 Mansion House speech.

Ingram, Mary, *A Jacobite Stronghold of the Church*. Edinburgh: R. Grant & Son, 1907.

Innes, A. D., *A History of the British Nation from the Earliest Times to the Present Day*. London and Edinburgh: T. C. and E. C. Jack, 1912.

Insh, George Pratt, *The Scottish Jacobite Movement*. Edinburgh and London, 1952.

Isaac, D. G. D., 'A Study of Popular Disturbances in Britain 1714–54'. Unpublished Ph.D. thesis, University of Edinburgh, 1953.

Jackson, Alvin, 'Unionist Myths 1912–1985'. *Past and Present* 136 (1992), 164–85.

The Jacobite. Summer 1988.

Jacobites or Covenanters: Which Tradition? A Scottish Republican Debate. n.p.: Scottish Republican Forum, 1994.

Jarvis, Rupert C., *The Jacobite Risings of 1715 and 1745*. Carlisle: Cumberland County Council Record Series no. 1, 1954.

Jenkins, David, *The British: Their Identity and Their Religion*. London: SCM Press, 1975.

Jones, Clyve (ed.), *Britain in the First Age of Party 1680–1750: Essays Presented to Geoffrey Holmes*. London and Ronceverte: Hambledon Press, 1987.

Jones, George Hilton, *The Main Stream of Jacobitism*. Cambridge, MA: Harvard University Press, 1954.

Keith, Alexander, *A Thousand Years of Aberdeen*. Aberdeen: Aberdeen University Press, 1972.

Kemp, Hilary, *The Jacobite Rebellion*. London: Almark Publishing, 1975.

Kidd, Colin, *Subverting Scotland's Past*. Cambridge: Cambridge University Press, 1993.

—— 'The Canon of Patriotic Landmarks in Scottish History'. *Scotlands* 1 (1994), 1–17.

Kington, Miles, *Punch on Scotland*. London: Punch Publications, 1977.

Kinsley, James, 'A Dryden Play at Edinburgh'. *Scottish Historical Review* 33 (1954), 129–32.

Kybett, Susan Maclean, *Bonnie Prince Charlie*. London, 1988.

Lang, Andrew, 'Jacobite Songs: *The True Loyalist or Chevalier's Favourite*, 1779'. *Scottish Historical Review* 8 (1911), 132–48.

Langford, Paul, *A Polite and Commercial People: England 1727–1783*. The New Oxford History of England. Oxford: Clarendon Press, 1989.

Langhorne, W. H., *Reminiscences*. Edinburgh: David Douglas, 1893.

Lathbury, Thomas, *A History of the Non-Jurors*. London: William Pickering, 1845.

Lawson, John Parker, *History of the Scottish Episcopal Church from the Revolution to the Present Time*. Edinburgh and London, 1843.

Leneman, Leah, *Living in Atholl 1685–1785*. Edinburgh: Edinburgh University Press, 1986.

Lenman, Bruce, *The Jacobite Risings in Britain 1689–1746*. London: Methuen, 1980.

—— *Integration, Enlightenment and Industrialization: Scotland 1746–1832*. The New History of Scotland 6. London: Edward Arnold, 1981.

—— *The Jacobite Clans of the Great Glen, 1650–1784*. London: Methuen, 1984.

—— 'A Client Society: Scotland between the '15 and the '45', in Jeremy Black (ed.), *Britain in the Age of Walpole*. London: Macmillan, 1984.

—— *The Jacobite Cause*. Glasgow: Richard Drew and National Trust for Scotland, 1986.

—— 'The Scottish Nobility and the Revolution of 1688–90', in Robert

Beddard (ed.), *The Revolutions of 1688.* Oxford: Clarendon Press, 1991, 137ff.

Linklater, Magnus and Christian Hesketh, *For King and Conscience: John Graham of Claverhouse, Viscount Dundee (1648–1689).* London: Weidenfeld & Nicolson, 1989.

Llewellyn, Nigel, *The Art of Death: Visual Culture in the English Death Ritual c1500–c1800.* London: Published in Association with the Victoria and Albert Museum by Reaktion Books, 1991.

Logue, Kenneth John, 'Popular Disturbances in Scotland 1780–1815'. Unpublished Ph.D. thesis. University of Edinburgh, 1977.

Lynch, Michael, *Scotland: A New History.* London: Century, 1991.

McBain, J. M., *Arbroath: Past & Present.* Arbroath: Brodie & Salmond, Brothock Bridge, 1887.

MacBean, W. M., 'A Contribution towards Jacobite Iconography'. MacBean Collection, Aberdeen University Special Collections.

McCann, Jean, 'The Organisation of the Jacobite Army, 1745–46'. Unpublished Ph.D. thesis. University of Edinburgh, 1963.

McCarthy, Justin, *A History of the Four Georges.* 4 vols. London: Chatto & Windus, 1890.

McCrone, David, Stephen Kendrick and Pat Shaw (eds), *The Making of Scotland: Nation, Culture and Social Change.* Edinburgh: Edinburgh University Press/British Sociological Association, 1989.

MacDonell, A. C., *Lays of the Heather: Poems.* London: Elliot Stock, 1896.

MacDougall, Hugh A., *Racial Myth in English History.* Montreal: Harvest House; Hanover, NH and London: University Press of New England, 1982.

Macfarlane, Charles and Thomas Thomson, *The Comprehensive History of England.* 4 vols. Oxford, Glasgow, Edinburgh and London: Blackie & Son, 1861.

MacInnes, Malcolm, *The 'Forty-Five: A Dramatised Account of the Jacobite Rising of 1745.* Paisley: Alexander Gardner, 1923.

Mackenzie, John M. (ed.), *Imperialism and Popular Culture.* Manchester: Manchester University Press, 1986.

Mackintosh, Alexander, *The Muster Roll of the Forfarshire or Lord Ogilvy's Regiment.* Inverness: The Northern Counties Newspaper & Printing & Publishing Co., 1914.

Mackintosh, A. M., *Brigadier Mackintosh of Borlum: Jacobite Hero and Martyr.* Nairn: George Bain, 1918.

Maclean, Sir Fitzroy, *A Concise History of Scotland.* London: Thames & Hudson, 1988 (1970).

McLynn, Frank, 'An Eighteenth-Century Scots Republic? – An Unlikely

Project from Absolutist France'. *Scottish Historical Review* 59 (1980), 177–81.

—— 'Reading History: Jacobites and the Jacobite Risings'. *History Today* (January 1983), 45–7.

—— *The Jacobite Army in England: The Final Campaign.* Edinburgh: John Donald, 1983.

—— *The Jacobites.* London: Routledge and Kegan Paul, 1985.

—— *Charles Edward Stuart.* London: Routledge, 1988.

—— *Crime and Punishment in Eighteenth-Century England.* London: Routledge, 1989.

MacNeill, D. H., 'Scottish and English Jacobites'. *Scots Independent* 167 (1941).

Martin, Raymond, 'Objectivity and Meaning in Historical Studies: Towards a Post-Analytic View'. *History and Theory* 32:1 (1993), 25–50.

Mason, Roger, 'Scotching the Brut: Politics, History and National Myth in Sixteenth-Century Britain', in idem (ed.) *Scotland and England 1286–1815.* Edinburgh: John Donald, 1983.

Mathieson, William Law, *Scotland and the Union: A History of Scotland from 1695 to 1747.* Glasgow: John Maclehose and Sons, 1905.

—— *The Awakening of Scotland.* Glasgow, 1910.

Meiklejohn, Professor J. M. D., *A New History of England and Great Britain.* 17th edn. London: Alfred Holden, 1902.

Millar, A. H., 'Killiecrankie Described by an Eye-Witness'. *Scottish Historical Review* 3 (1906), 63–70.

Miller, John, 'Catholic Officers in the Later Stuart Army'. *English Historical Review* 88 (1973), 35–53.

Mingay, G. E., *English Landed Society in the Eighteenth Century.* London: Routledge & Kegan Paul; Toronto: University of Toronto Press, 1963.

Mitchison, Rosalind, 'Patriotism and National Identity in Eighteenth-century Scotland', in T. W. Moody (ed.), Historical Studies, XI: *Nationality and the Pursuit of National Independence.* Belfast: The Appletree Press, for the Irish Committee of Historical Studies, 1978, 94ff.

Monod, Paul, 'The Politics of Matrimony', in Eveline Cruickshanks and Jeremy Black (eds), *The Jacobite Challenge.* Edinburgh: John Donald, 1988.

—— *Jacobitism and the English People.* Cambridge: Cambridge University Press, 1989.

—— 'Dangerous Merchandise: Smuggling, Jacobitism and Commercial Culture in Southeast England'. *Journal of British Studies* 30:2 (1991), 150–82.

Moody-Stuart, Major K. A., 'Lieutenant-Colonel James Steuart: A

Jacobite Lieutenant-Governor of Edinburgh Castle'. *Scottish Historical Review* 21 (1924), 1–25.

Murdoch-Lawrence, R., 'Aberdeen Women as Jacobites'. *Aberdeen Journal: Notes and Queries* 1 (1908), 49.

Murray, W. H., *Rob Roy MacGregor: His Life and Times*. Edinburgh: Canongate, 1993 (1982).

Nairn, Tom, *The Break-Up of Britain*. London: NLB, 1977.

—— *The Enchanted Glass*. London: Radius, 1988.

Newman, Gerald, *The Rise of English Nationalism: A Cultural History 1740–1830*. London: Weidenfeld & Nicolson, 1987.

Ó Buachalla, Breandan, 'Irish Jacobitism in Official Documents'. *Eighteenth-Century Ireland* 8 (1993), 128–38.

O'Halloran, Clare, 'Irish Re-creations of the Gaelic Past: The Challenge of Macpherson's Ossian'. *Past and Present* 124 (1989), 69–95.

Oliphant, T. L. Kingston, *The Jacobite Lairds of Gask*. The Grampian Club. London: Charles Griffin and Co., 1870.

Omond, G. W. T., *The Early History of the Scottish Union Question*. Edinburgh and London: Oliphant Anderson & Ferrier, 1897.

Opie, Robert, *Rule Britannia: Trading on the British Image*. Harmondsworth: Penguin, 1985.

Osmond, John, *The Divided Kingdom*. A Channel Four Book. London: Constable, 1988.

Ouston, Hugh, 'York in Edinburgh: James VII and the Patronage of Learning in Scotland, 1679–1688', in John Dwyer, Roger A. Mason and Alexander Murdoch (eds), *New Perspectives on the Politics and Culture of Early Modern Scotland*. Edinburgh: John Donald, n.d. (c. 1983).

Paterson, Lindsay, *The Autonomy of Modern Scotland*. Edinburgh: Edinburgh University Press, 1994.

Perry, The Very Rev. W., *The Oxford Movement in Scotland*. Cambridge: Cambridge University Press, 1933.

Phillipson, Nicholas, *Hume*. London: Weidenfeld & Nicolson, 1989.

Pittock, Murray G. H., 'Decadence and the English Tradition'. Unpublished D.Phil. thesis. Oxford University, 1986.

—— 'Jacobitism in the North-East: The Pitsligo Papers in Aberdeen University Library', in J. J. Carter and J. H. Pittock (eds), *Aberdeen and the Enlightenment*. Aberdeen: Aberdeen University Press, 1987, 69–76.

—— 'New Jacobite Songs of the Forty-five'. *Studies in Voltaire and the Eighteenth Century* 267 (1989), 1–75.

—— *The Invention of Scotland: The Stuart Myth and the Scottish Identity, 1638 to the Present*. London and New York: Routledge, 1991.

—— *Clio's Clavers*. Edinburgh: Leerie Books, 1992.

—— 'Sources and Dates for the Jacobite Song'. *Archives* (1993), 25–9.

—— 'Scott as Historiographer: The Case of *Waverley*', in D. S. Hewitt and J. H. Alexander (eds), *Scott in Carnival*. Aberdeen: Association for Scottish Literary Studies, 1993, 145–53.

—— *Poetry and Jacobite Politics in Eighteenth-Century Britain and Ireland*. Cambridge: Cambridge University Press, 1994.

—— 'Forging North Britain in the Age of Macpherson'. *Edinburgh Review* (Spring 1995), forthcoming.

—— 'Jacobite Culture'. In 'Charlie's Year'. HMSO; Glasgow Museums, forthcoming.

—— 'From Edinburgh to London: Scottish Court Writing and 1603'. *Studies in Voltaire and the Eighteenth Century*, forthcoming.

Pocock, J. G. A., 'British History: A Plea for a New Subject'. *Journal of Modern History* 47:4 (1975), 601–21 (responses 626–8).

—— 'The Limits and Divisions of British History: In Search of an Unknown Subject'. *American Historical Review* 87 (1982), 311–36.

Pollard, A. F., *The History of England: A Study in Political Evolution*. London: Williams and Norgate, n.d.

Prebble, John, *Culloden*. London: Secker & Warburg, 1961.

—— *The King's Jaunt*. London, 1988.

Rayner, Robert M., *A Concise History of Britain*. Complete Edition in One Volume. London, New York and Toronto: Longmans, Green and Co., 1941.

Richards, Thomas, *The Commodity Culture of Victorian England*. Stanford: Stanford University Press, 1990.

Riley, P. W. J., *The Union of England and Scotland*. Manchester: Manchester University Press, 1978.

Robertson, F. W., 'Re-Appraising the Forty-Five', *Scots Independent* 1944 (4).

—— *The Scottish Way 1746–1946: Freedom's Decline – and the Truth about the Highland Clans*. Rothesay, 1946.

Robertson, John, *The Scottish Enlightenment and the Militia Issue*. Edinburgh: John Donald, 1985.

Robinson, Cyril, *England: A History of British Progress from the Early Ages to the Present Day*. London: Methuen, 1929.

Robinson, I. S., 'Pope Gregory VII, the Princes and the Pactum 1077–1080'. *English Historical Review* 94 (1979), 721–56.

Rose, Craig, ' "Seminarys of Faction and Rebellion": Jacobites, Whigs and the London Charity Schools, 1716–1724'. *Historical Journal* 34 (1991), 831–55.

Rosie, George, 'Museumry and the Heritage Industry', in Ian Donnachie and Christopher Whatley (eds), *The Manufacture of Scottish History*. Edinburgh: Polygon, 1992, 157–70.

Samuel, Raphael (ed.), *Patriotism: The Making and Unmaking of British National Identity*. 3 vols. London and New York: Routledge, 1989.

Samuel, Raphael and Paul Thompson (eds), *The Myths We Live By*. London and New York: Routledge, 1990.

Schuddehopf, Otto-Ernst, Edouard Bruley, E. H. Dance and Haakon Vigander, *History Teaching and History Textbook Revision*. Strasbourg: Centre for Cultural Co-operation of the Council of Europe, 1967.

The Scots Independent 1927–54.

Scottish Notes and Queries vols 1, 5ff. (1887ff.).

Scott-Moncrieff, Lesley (ed.), *The '45: To Gather an Image Whole*. Edinburgh: The Mercat Press, 1988.

See, Henri and Alexander Cormack, 'Commercial Relations between France and Scotland in 1707'. *Scottish Historical Review* 23 (1926), 275–9.

Seton, Sir Bruce, Bart, 'Dress of the Jacobite Army'. *Scottish Historical Review* 25 (1928), 270–81.

Sharpe, J. A., '"Last Dying Speeches": Religion, Ideology and Public Execution in Seventeenth-Century England'. *Past and Present* 107 (1985), 144–67.

Shaw, Lachlan, *The History of the Province of Moray*. 3 vols. Glasgow: Glasgow University Press; London: Hamilton, Adams & Co.; Glasgow: Thomas D. Morison, 1882.

Sinclair-Stevenson, Christopher, *Inglorious Rebellion: The Jacobite Risings of 1708, 1715 and 1719*. London: Hamish Hamilton, 1971.

Smith, Annette, 'Dundee and the '45', in Lesley Scott-Moncreiff (ed.), *The '45: To Gather an Image Whole*. Edinburgh: The Mercat Press, 1988, 99–112.

Speck, W. A., 'Will the Real 18th Century Stand Up?' *Historical Journal* 34 (1991), 203–6.

Springhall, John, '"Up Guards and at Them!": British Imperialism and Popular Art, 1880–1914', in John M. Mackenzie (ed.), *Imperialism and Popular Culture*. Manchester: Manchester University Press, 1986, 49–72.

Stafford, Fiona, *The Sublime Savage*. Edinburgh: Edinburgh University Press, 1988.

Steele, Margaret, 'Anti-Jacobite Pamphleteering, 1701–1720'. *Scottish Historical Review* 60 (1981), 140–55.

Steuart, A. Francis, *Patrick Lindesay the Jacobite: Founded on his Letters in the Possession of the Earl of Lindsay*. Edinburgh: Douglas & Fachs, 1927.

Stevenson, David, *The Scottish Revolution 1637–1644*. Newton Abbot: David & Charles, 1973.

—— *Revolution and Counter-Revolution in Scotland 1644–1657*. London: Royal Historical Society, 1977.

Stone, Lawrence, 'The Revival of Narrative: Reflections on a New Old History'. *Past and Present* 85 (1979), 3–24.

—— 'History and Post-Modernism'. *Past and Present* 131 (1989), 217–18.

Sweeney-Turner, Steve, 'Music Fyne: More Parcels of Rogues'. *Cencrastus* 50 (1994/95), 29.

Szechi, Daniel, *Jacobitism and Tory Politics 1710–14*. Edinburgh: John Donald, 1984.

—— *The Jacobites*. Manchester: Manchester University Press, 1994.

Szechi, Daniel and David Hayton, 'John Bull's Other Kingdoms: The English Government of Scotland and Ireland', in Clyve Jones (ed.), *Britain in the First Age of Party 1680–1750*. London and Ronceverte: Hambledon Press, 1987.

Tayler, Alistair and Henrietta Tayler, *Jacobites of Aberdeenshire and Banffshire in the Forty-Five*. Aberdeen: Milne & Hutchison, 1928.

—— *Jacobites of Aberdeenshire and Banffshire in the Rising of 1715*. Edinburgh and London: Oliver & Boyd, 1934.

—— *1715: The Story of the Rising*. London and Edinburgh: Thomas Nelson, 1936.

—— 'The Jacobites of Buchan', in J. F. Tocher (ed.), *The Book of Buchan (Jubilee Volume)*. Aberdeen: Aberdeen University Press; Peterhead: P. Scrogie, 1943.

Tayler, Henrietta, 'John Gordon of Glenbucket'. *Scottish Historical Review* 27 (1948), 165–75.

Taylor, Miles, 'John Bull and the Iconography of Public Opinion in England c. 1712–1929'. *Past and Present* 134 (1990), 93–128.

Taylor, Philip M., *The Projection of Britain: British Overseas Publicity and Propaganda 1919–1939*. Cambridge: Cambridge University Press, 1981.

Terry, Charles Sanford, 'The Battle of Glenshiel'. *Scottish Historical Review* 2 (1905), 412–23.

—— *The Jacobites and the Union*. Cambridge: Cambridge University Press, 1922.

Thom, Walter, *The History of Aberdeen*. 2 vols. Aberdeen: D. Chalmers, 1811.

Thomson, James, *The History of Dundee*. Dundee: John Durkan & Son, 1874.

Tocher, J. F. (ed.), *The Book of Buchan (Jubilee Volume)*. Aberdeen: Aberdeen University Press; Peterhead: P. Scrogie, 1943.

Trench, Charles Chevenix, *George II*. London: Allen Lane, 1973.

Trevelyan, G. M., *England Under the Stuarts*. Volume 5 of *A History of England* in 8 volumes, general editor Sir Charles Oman KBE. 19th edn. London: Methuen, 1947 (1904).

—— *History of England*. 3rd edn. London, New York and Toronto: Longman, Green & Co., 1952 (1945).

Trevor-Roper, Hugh, 'The Invention of Tradition: The Highland Tradition of Scotland', in Eric Hobsbawm and Terence Ranger (eds), *The Invention of Tradition*. Cambridge: Cambridge University Press, 1983, 15–41.

Turnbull, Michael (ed.), *The Poems of John Davidson*. 2 vols. Edinburgh: Scottish Academic Press, 1973.

White, Gavin, 'The Consecration of Bishop Seabury'. *Scottish Historical Review* 63 (1984), 37–49.

Williams, A. M., 'Sir George Mackenzie of Rosehaugh'. *Scottish Historical Review* 13 (1916), 138–48.

Williams, Basil, *The Whig Supremacy 1714–1760*. Volume XI of the *Oxford History of England*, ed. G. N. Clark. Oxford: Clarendon Press, 1952 (1939).

Womack, Peter, *Improvement and Romance: Constructing the Myth of the Highlands*. Basingstoke: Macmillan, 1989.

Wood, Stephen, *The Scottish Soldier*. Manchester: National Museums of Scotland, Archive Publications, 1987.

—— *The Auld Alliance: Scotland and France, the Military Connection*. Edinburgh: Mainstream, 1989.

Woolf, D. R., 'The "Common Voice": History, Folklore and Oral Tradition in Early Modern England'. *Past and Present* 120 (1988), 26–52.

Young, James, 'Forging the Nation'. *Cencrastus* 49 (1994), 40–1.

Index

disaffection in, 67
Jacobite support in 1745, 61–4, 67, 74
population of, 58
Britannia, 21, 30
British identity, 20–2, 121
and Sir Walter Scott, 25
Bruce, Robert
and ethnicity, 26
ideological significance of, 34
in song, 109
Burke, Edmund, 21, 115
Butterfield, Herbert, 1, 4, 17

Caesaro-sacramentalism, 49
Cameronians, and Jacobitism, 95–6
cannibalism, and the Scots, 9
Carlyle, Alexander, 32
Catholicism
alien quality of, 21
in Buchan, 48
attitude to Gaelic, 56
and Jacobitism, 30
in Kincardine O'Neil, 48
celticism, 21, 26, 36, 37, 39
Charles I, and Anglo–Scottish relations, 91
Charles II, and Anglo–Scottish relations, 91
Chasing the Deer, 3
Chatterton, Thomas, 37
Clearances, 27, 41, 112
Clifton, Francis, 108
Colley, Linda, 13, 21, 84
and James Macpherson, 38
Cotton, Sir John Hynde, and tartan, 55
Covenanting army
size of, 46
strength of, 59
support in localities, 71–8
Culloden, Battle of (1746), National Trust for Scotland Battlefield Centre, 4, 7–8

Davidson, John, 26
deer, and the Clearances, 27
Diamond Jubilee (1897), 119
Disruption, 34
dress of Jacobite army, 55–6
Dundas, Henry, and opposition to Union, 114
Dundee
Jacobite support in 1715, 52

Jacobite support in 1745, 60–4, 65–6, 73–4
Jacobite compared with Covenanting support, 73–4
social background of Jacobite support, 83
Dundee, Viscount (John Graham of Claverhouse), 79
army of, 43–5, 54, 59

East Lothian, Jacobite support in, 64
Edinburgh
assessment under Press Act, 80
disaffection in, 86
Episcopacy in, 65, 69–70
Jacobite activity in, 53, 64
Jacobite support in 1745, 60, 64, 69–70
James VII's court in, 91
population of, 69
social background of Jacobite recruits, 82
town guard, sympathies of in 1745, 64
Edinburgh (county)
Jacobite support in, 70
population of, 58
Edward VII, 3
Elgin (county)
assessment in Press Act, 80
Jacobite support in 1745, 61–2
English identity, 19, 21, 24–5, 30–1, 34
and Germanic roots, 21, 24–6, 30–1
Enlightenment, in Scotland, 32, 38
Episcopal Church
and Anglicanism, 104–5
and Charles Edward Stuart, 65
attitude to Gaelic, 56
distribution of in 1708, 47
in Edinburgh, 65, 69–70
historiography of, 100–2
history of, 46–7, 104–5
ideology of, 17, 30, 103–4
and Jacobite song, 106
and Jacobitism, 83–4, 93
and James VIII, 102
local strength of, 47
modern composition of, 104–5
and nationalism, 93, 97–8, 102
in Perthshire, 76
relations with Catholicism, 48–9
relations with Lutheranism, 49